ISBN 978-1-331-58205-2
PIBN 10208753

1 MONTH OF
FREE
READING

at

www.ForgottenBooks.com

By purchasing this book you are eligible for one month membership to ForgottenBooks.com, giving you unlimited access to our entire collection of over 700,000 titles via our web site and mobile apps.

To claim your free month visit:

www.forgottenbooks.com/free208753

English
Français
Deutsche
Italiano
Español
Português

www.forgottenbooks.com

Mythology Photography **Fiction**
Fishing Christianity **Art** Cooking
Essays Buddhism Freemasonry
Medicine **Biology** Music **Ancient**
Egypt Evolution Carpentry Physics
Dance Geology **Mathematics** Fitness
Shakespeare **Folklore** Yoga Marketing
Confidence Immortality Biographies
Poetry **Psychology** Witchcraft
Electronics Chemistry History **Law**
Accounting **Philosophy** Anthropology
Alchemy Drama Quantum Mechanics
Atheism Sexual Health **Ancient History**
Entrepreneurship Languages Sport
Paleontology Needlework Islam
Metaphysics Investment Archaeology
Parenting Statistics Criminology
Motivational

THE CHASTISEMENT OF

MAN

By

Hector France

Translated by ALFRED ALLINSON

FRONTISPIECE BY J. WELY (OF PARIS)

PARIS

Charles Carrington

13 Faubourg Montmartre 13

1898

PREFACE

To Camille Delthil

On horseback, riding among my comrades of the red
cavalry, I jotted down the first outlines of this book.
Then I forgot all about the flying leaves that, burned
brown by the sun, stained by rain and damp, frayed
against the saddle, torn and tumbled, lost in cantonments
and found again, had lain by me so long.

But on an evening in December, when the London fog
hung heavy on the lungs, entering—and the English *spleen*
along with it—at every chink and crevice of ill-fitting
door or window, I was fain to forget a while my exile
and my surroundings and the inexorable flight of time.

And like a mare that heat of blood spurs on, my
thought burst its shackles and escaped, and fled to the
wide spaces of the past, tracing the days gone by to the
far-off horizon where the sky shines blue.

Ah! the wild gallops down the valleys and between the
hills where dwarf-oaks grow and olives, pomegranates and
cactus; the merry rides over the plain, following the long
line of oleanders that clothe with their graceful festoons
the sterile river-banks of crumbling chalk; the long halts
under the bushy tamarinds beside the cool spring, whither
the dark-eyed maids of the desert come to draw water.
Then again on the outskirts of those vast solitudes that

the caravans penetrate, the mad hunts after the gazelles, while far away against the horizon blazing with the glow of sunset, the white profile of the minaret of the *Ksour* and the tangled heads of the date-palms of the Oasis tremble in the transparent air.

I collected the papers, and during long night hours, when the cold north-wind rattled at my door, I would stop my ears, and ensconced in my dreams, caressed by the golden rays of memory, obliterate the present, and live wholly in the past.

Puritans who have been scandalized by my other books, may take heart of grace and be re-assured. They will find no dangerous matters touched on here.

Here are pictures of pastoral life, which I dedicate to you, my poet! I speak here of Nature, that you love, of wide desert solitudes, of black-haired maids and golden harvests; I tell the tale of rude, simple-hearted loves, such as you sing in your "Poèmes Rustiques", such as your compatriot and our friend, Léon Cladel, has thrown,—a garland of wild flowers, round the granite plinth of his rugged "Paysans".

But it is not along cool woodland paths, "all bathed in morning-dew", I would guide your steps, where:

> A child and fancy-free,
> Singing in simple glee
> She goes; you love to see
> Her face
> And rustic grace.
>
> She bears in antique pose
> Her amphora; and knows
> Nothing of worldly shows,—
> And yet
> A born coquette!

Rather would I lead you over vast, bare plains, the land of the palm-tree, the land where the rustic child of nature, clad in the tunic of Rebecca, offers in trusting innocence her bosom, her arms, her limbs, naked to the sun's kisses. I would introduce you to the tent of skins where dwell the peasants of the *Tell*, more stately under their ragged *burnouse* than ever were patricians the most noble, to the home of the peaceful, pastoral *Bedouins*, whom the sabre of conquering civilization, has so often and so suddenly swooped down upon to awaken them from their quiet dreams and old-world loves.

HECTOR FRANCE.

PROLOGUE

I told you all,
When we first put this dangerous stone a-rolling
'Twould fall upon ourselves.

KING HENRY VIII. *Act V. Sc. 2.*

PROLOGUE

ON the horizon, blue hills that fringe the curtain of the setting sun with their gently undulating outlines; beyond them the sky all a-blaze as with the conflagration of some titanic City of the Plain, the reflections of its furnace-fires reddening the lofty cloud-crests of the Eastern heavens.

The lurid light was still about us, as we rode; but the desert was already darkening under the on-coming shadows of night. Darkness, deep and impenetrable, was creeping over the plain and hiding every detail,—wild sombre ravines, burnt patches of barren earth, green clumps of brushwood, sand-hills piled by the wind, the dark surface of the swamps of *Ain-Chabrou*, the laurels hanging precariously to the crumbling slopes along the course of the torrent and reflected in its brown waters, the long white ribbon of the track winding deviously towards the palm-trees of the *Ksour*.

The *Ksour!—Djenarah*, the pearl of the *Souf!* From the mountain slopes of the *Djebel*, my guide had pointed out its lofty minaret, rising like a slender mast of alabaster amid the blue waves of the distant horizon. For miles we watched its white needle-like shaft glittering in the rays of the setting sun. Little by little it disappeared from sight, as we descended into the plain and were engulfed in the gloom.

Indistinct shapes would suddenly cross our path; and giant bats, darting from the ravines, fluttered round our heads.

Now and again two glowing sparks would shine out in some dark thicket, and the deep covert by the road-side shake with a low rustling sound.

The desert was peopled with invisible foes, the silence broken by weird, mysterious noises. I was listening mechanically to the heavy, monotonous beat, beat of the horses' hoofs, as they paced wearily over the stony soil, and the shrill croaking of the marsh-frogs that now and again reached our ears from the bottom of the valley, when my Spahi's voice broke the dreary spell, bursting gaily into song:

> From Skikdad to Constantine,
> From Constantine to Bathna,
> Who's the maid of the gayest mien,
> Of all the maids of Fathma?
> >'Tis Kreïra!
> >My Kreïra!
> 'Tis Kreïra, my peerless queen,
> 'Tis the rose-bud of Ouargla!

One of the wanton love-songs the Arabs delight in, and which they sing on weary journeys, when hour after hour plain succeeds to plain, and the eye can find nothing to relieve the grey monotony of the sun-baked sand but the blue of the distant horizon that ever flies before the wayfarer as he advances.

We had but just reached the level of the plain, and I was dozing in the saddle, my senses lulled at once by the Spahi's song and by the regular movement of my horse, when far away across the silence of the desert I seemed to hear cries of distress.

"Hush!" I cried to Salah.

I was not mistaken. Again the same cry was raised,—solemn, mournful, dreary. No single word reached us clearly, but the tone of despair, sounding through the night, was inexpressibly sad.

The voice ceased; and deep silence fell upon the desert. Beasts and reptiles, all the host of creatures that prowl by night, seemed to stand still and listen.

"Did you hear it?"

"Oh! yes," replied the Spahi; and again struck up:

> 'Twixt her bosoms as I lie,
> Eyes a-swoon, all drunk with love,
> Peerless houri! shall I sigh
> For the joys of Heaven above?
>   O! Kreïra!
>   My Kreïra!
> O! Kreïra, the flower of love,
> The fairest rose of Ouargla!

"Silence!" I cried again indignantly. "Some one calls for help."

"I know. There is nothing to be done. 'Tis the voice of *Sidi-Messaoud* (My Lord the Happy Man)."

The Happy Man! The irony of it! My heart was stirred by the grim cry ringing from afar like the dying echoes of some calamitous disaster. Who can *the happy man* be that groans so unhappily?

We pursued our way, and though an hour and more had elapsed, my thoughts still obstinately refused to leave the spot where I had heard the mournful cry. Salah continued his love-song, couplet after couplet, as if he could never weary; but of a sudden he stopped.

The voice rang out again nearer than before; and we could distinguish a name sobbed forth. We heard it plainly, three times repeated:

"Afsia! Afsia! Afsia!"

The cry was heart-rending. For a moment it seemed to touch the Spahi, piercing even the soldier's rude exterior, for he drew rein and stopped.

I could see his shadow, big and black, relieved against the grey of the sandy road, musket resting across the *Kerbouk* of his saddle, and sabre under thigh, the steel scabbard and hilt of copper glittering in the surrounding darkness.

His head wrapped in his pointed hood, the *burnouse* wound tightly round his body, he sat leaning forward in the saddle, motionless and thoughtful.

"What is it? what does it mean?" I asked him, when for the third time the despairing accents fell silent again. "Who is it calls at this hour of the night and in the lonely desert?"

"'Tis nothing that need trouble you," he answered, and laughed. "It is Sidi-Messaoud calling for his bride."

And he struck up his song once more:

> Her lips are a cup of pleasure,
> Brimmed full of blood-red wine;
> Pressed to her bosom's treasure,
> To die were bliss divine,
>   With Kreïra,
>   Fair Kreïra,
> With Kreïra, were she mine, were she mine,—
> Were she mine, the rose of Ouargla!

I could draw nothing further from him; and during my sojourn at the Ksour the men of Djenarah always found one excuse or another for not answering my enquiries on the subject. Presently amidst the manifold events of a soldier's life in Africa the recollection faded from my memory.

It was not till several years later, on my return to Constantine, that by mere chance I heard from the *Thaleb* El-Hadj-Ali-bou-Nahr the tragic history of *The Happy Man.*

The *Thaleb*, Ali-bou-Nahr, enjoying the honourable title of El-Hadj, as do' all Mussulmans who have made the pilgrimage to Mecca, was a familiar figure with all the French Spahis in Africa,—all I mean who were quartered at Constantine about the year 1860. At that time we occupied the barracks of *Sidi-Nemdil*, in the very centre of the native town, and immediately opposite a small, picturesque mosque, that has long since vanished before the pickaxe of improvement.

The Thaleb had established himself within a few yards of our doors. His business was to hire out his pen and the charms of his style to illiterate lovers, to copy out for sale verses from the Koran in his beautiful handwriting, to cup patients in need of his assistance,—and the sale of amulets. In other words he was at one and the same time scrivener, barber, surgeon and in a mild way, sorcerer.

Ali-bou-Nahr was a man of honourable life and high repute for wisdom. He was well-read in philosophy and letters; and on returning from Mecca had travelled in several European countries. A devout man, he would quote the Koran with unction, but like the English Puritans with the Bible, he had his own interpretations of its meaning. He observed the great fast of Ramadan to outward appearance, and never drank wine—till after dark.

"The Laws of the Prophet," he would say, "are made for the vulgar. *We* are wise men ; *our* law is our conscience. Still appearances must be kept up, for the sake of the ignorant masses. If the Koran did not forbid wine, every camel-driver would lie drunk by the roadside."

The sale of amulets was, as I have said, a part of his business,—and the most lucrative part. Did a man encounter a big toad at moonrise lying in ambush by the roadside, or a tiny snake lurking in the grass and darting at him a glance of its evil yellow eyes, his first thought was to apply to a seller of charms, and for choice to Ali-bou-Nahr.

Every good woman from Philippeville to Tuggurt, every herdsman of the Tell, every camel-owner of the Souf, every ass-driver of Constantine, knows that the *Djenouns* (Demons of the Night) choose these shapes in preference to all others so as to shoot their poison the more readily at the unsuspecting wayfarer. Then, woe to him ! unless he run with all haste to the nearest *Marabout*, or failing him to his neighbour the *Tebib*, to buy a talisman,—the only antidote against the Evil One.

The magic formula is traced on a little square of paper, linen or parchment, of the same size and shape as the sacred scapularies of our own monks.

The patient fastens it reverently with a cord round his neck, and—always provided he have faith, the remedy is infallible.

There are charms for all diseases and all evil spells. They are sovereign against the itch and the plague, sudden death and ophthalmia, foul women and unfaithful wives, bullets and vermin. All depends on the price.

" Strange ! Men call you learned," I would say to him,
" and a sage ; yet you are not ashamed to trade thus on
the folly of the vulgar."

" My son !" the Thaleb would reply, " you speak after
the fashion of the unbelievers, who ever use swelling
words to hide the emptiness of their thoughts. Did I make
the vulgar fools? Nay! they are fools from the beginning,
and it is but right their folly, like other human weak-
nesses, should be turned to the advantage of the wise and
learned. The physician is not the cause of fever and
ophthalmia; but he lives by them. He lives by the drugs
that kill, and the lotions that make men one-eyed. I
live by my amulets; if they do not cure folly, at least
they cure the mischief folly causes. We are all of us, my
son, charlatans more or less.

" The physician is a scientific charlatan, the magistrate a
moral one, the soldier is a charlatan in gallantry, the
priest in virtue. Each of them lives by his trade; let me
live by mine. The sun shines for all alike; but so long
as the mass of men remains stupid and ignorant, they
will continue to be the victims of the more astute."

Like every true Mussulman, Ali-bou-Nahr entertained a
profound contempt for all Christians,—not because they
were Christians, but because he held their religion to be
childish, narrow and absurd. If he honoured me with his
good opinion, it was because I chanced one day to declare
myself a fatalist and my belief that the Koran was far
preferable to the Gospel,—considering the delights of the
Mohamedan paradise.

" Yes !" he would say, " good men shall enjoy beauties
everlastingly virgin, streams everlastingly pure, shade ever-

lastingly cool and refreshing; is not this better than ever-lastingly to be singing hymns? The son of Abdallah understood human nature better than the son of Mary. But hymns or houris, all this appeals only, and applies only, to the common herd wise men despise.

"You believe in fatalism. Well and good! but the strong man can shape his course athwart the will of fate."

And he quoted these words from the Book:

"'They that do good, shall find good above measure. There shall be no blemish and no shame shall tarnish the brightness of their countenance. They that do evil, shall find retribution to match the evil; shamed-facedness shall cover them as with a garment, and their countenance shall be black as night.'

"It may well be that the short-sighted crowd will say, seeing only the surface of things: Behold yonder man; he makes his passions his god, he chooses evil for good, his heart is cold and his hand tight-shut, others' misery is his gain,—yet he flourishes exceedingly and waxes fat, he is finely clothed and luxuriously lodged, he is happy! Wait, short-sighted fools; and your eyes shall be opened, and you shall see punishment striding towards him with swift avenging steps. Retribution dogs his way. He shall bow his proud head to the ground, like a penitent that prays forgiveness for his crimes.

"For Fate, when its hour has come, stays not to chastise till the flesh be loosened from the bones, but strikes the evil-doer in his might.

"I know one whom the folk of the Tell, and of the Souf, and of the Sahara, have for long years surnamed *The Happy Man;* and he is an object of pity to the meanest and the most unfortunate."

"Ah!" I exclaimed, "I remember. Once, not far from Djenarah, I heard his voice. *Afsia! Afsia! Afsia!* he cried. The name has long haunted my memory."

And whilst I told my tale, he listened gloomily, only interrupting me to interject: *Allah Kebir! Allah Kebir!* (God is Great!)

When I had finished, he said:

"Come this evening, and bring two goat-skins of the good wine of Spain that makes the heart laugh. Safe from slandering tongues and prying eyes, from the envy of men and the blandishments of women, behind the bolts and bars of my house, I will tell you the history of the *Thaleb El-Messaoud.*"

THE CHASTISEMENT OF MANSOUR

Love comforteth like sunshine after rain,
But lust's effect is tempest—after sun ;
Love's gentle spring doth always fresh remain,
Lust's-winter comes ere summer half be done ;
Love surfeits not ; lust like a glutton dies ;
Love is all truth ; lust full of forged lies.

VENUS AND ADONIS.

FIRST PART

MERYEM

To even her with greeny bough were vain;
Fool he who finds her beauties in the roe:
When hath the roe those lively lovely limbs
Or honey dews those lips alone bestow?
Those eyne, soul-piercing eyne, which slay with love,
Which bind the victim by their shafts laid low?
My heart to second childhood they beguiled;
No wonder: love-sick man again is child!

"**Arabian Nights**"
(BURTON'S TRANS.)

MERYEM

I.

"THERE is no God but God, and Mohammed is the Prophet of God."

"His are the East and the West; which way soever a man turneth himself, there shall he meet His face."

Such the words written in the Book, but I can tell a word that is not written,—what they amongst us that are called wise men rehearse.

There is God, and there is the Prophet; but between them is a Master, almighty. He it is that makes, and unmakes; he that gives light, and takes it away.

Some name him all-pervading Life; but his true name is Love all-pervading.

From man to mite, from towering palm-tree to lowly blade of alpha-grass, nought exists, nought lives, but by him. The World bends beneath his will, as the bull-rushes bend before the hurricane.

He scatters the races of mankind over the surface of the globe, as the sower scatters the grain over the seed-field.

His temple is the universe, its high altar woman; there is nothing more perfect our sun shines upon.

So in place of the words of the Prophet, we say :.

" *His* are the East and the West; and which way soever a man turneth himself, there shall he meet the power of Love."

He is the arbiter of all things, sorrow and joy, death and life. He makes us wise or foolish, happy or unfortunate, heroes or felons.

Without Love man is emasculate; as much a eunuch all his life through as the negro guards of the *Harem*.

True, to the weak he is a stumbling-block; but to the strong man he points the road and says: "I am on thy side, carve out thy destiny."

For the strong man, unless harassed and hampered by the accursed and fatal consequences of crime or cowardice on the part of the fathers whose blood flows in his veins, is master of his fate in this world of ours. He holds in his own hands good luck and ill. And on the threshold of old age, should cares settle down like the shades of night upon his head, let him blame none but himself, let him ransack the foul memories of his past to find the reason.

II.

THE men of Djenarah would not tell you the

story of the Thaleb *El-Hadj-Mansour El-Messaoud,*
for there are still living at the Ksour men and women
who have cause to blush at the mention of his
name. The doom that has fallen upon him is
terrible; but anger still survives in the hearts of
many. The more generous have forgiven him, but
even *they* cannot forget.

For me, I honour *Sidi-Mansour,* and respect his
misfortunes, and if God prolong my days after *his*
are ended, I shall offer at the tomb where his
ashes repose the gifts due to a great Marabout.

Yet this man, who it may be after death will be
revered as the equal of *Sidi-Ibrahim* or *Abd-el-
Kader,* was in his youth a great sinner.

They say he was full of cleverness,—as wise as
Satan. Every enterprise was crowned with success,
he was so cunning; but his enterprises were too
often evil.

Love was his pastime, and on it he lavished all
his skill and dauntless intrepidity. Who can count
the tale of husbands and fathers he deceived, of
wives cajoled and maidens dishonoured? Not even
the folk of Djenarah could tell them all; for a man
seldom knows his own shame.

Not alone Djenarah the Pearl, but the *douars*
(encampments, villages) of the Nememchas and the
Ouled-Abid, and the plains of the Souf to far away
Ouargla and Rhadamés, rang with the scandal of
his lawless loves.

His boast was: " No man is a match for me."

And it was true, for none could stay him in his dissolute courses.

When the old men of the city reproved him, and said:

"O Mansour! he who takes Satan for comrade, chooses a bad travelling companion," or "Mansour! a day will come when shame shall be spread about your head like a tent;" then, swollen with the pride of Eblis the Accursed (the Devil), he would answer: "I have but to lift my head, and burst through the shame; I am not of those that tamely bow the neck."

Then they would say: "Beware! it will be too late when at last you cry, *I repent!* Though you implore forgiveness seventy times, as it is written in the Book, though you invoke God by his ninety and nine names, it will be too late!"

"Remember the words of the Prophet,—'Soul for soul, eye for eye, nose for nose, ear for ear, tooth for tooth.' The law of retaliation is the law of God."

But he would answer, and laugh: 'Only God knows what to-morrow may bring forth!"

Beneath the tents of the *Beled-el-Djerid* (Country of Dates), as under the roofs of the Ksour, many a tale is told of his youthful adventures; and I will relate the first of them, for it affected all his after life.

O God!. blind the eyes of the wicked, tear his tongue from between his lips, cut his virility from between his thighs, that he may not beget others as wicked as himself. But have pity on him whose crimes have been expiated before the hour of his death!

III.

He was barely sixteen, but, already he understood how to clothe falsehood in the specious guise of truth. In other words he was a man. He was bold and enterprising, and his looks pleased the maidens of the tribe. He used his advantages to sow disorder broadcast,—to creep between loving hearts and disunite them.

His intrigues remained long undetected: for he was expert in keeping them a secret. But vague suspicions were rife.

At this time his father, *Ahmed-ben-Rahan*, Sheikh of the *Ouled-Ascars*, a subordinate tribe of the *Ouled-Sidi-Abid*, married his fourth wife.

The second and third wives had died more than a year before, and the first wife, the mother of Mansour, was left alone. Then she said to the Sheikh:

"My Lord! I grow old and weary. My thirty-fifth year draws nigh, and from the age of twenty I have been thy faithful slave, a humble and industrious wife to thee. Ever have I guarded as my most precious treasure what God bids a woman guard for her husband; and thou hast found no cause of complaint against me.

"God has blessed my bed with increase, for I

have borne thee a son—the handsomest and proudest youth of all the Ouled-Ascars. Now, listen! I am fain of rest. I will ever be thy handmaid and thy wife. But I pray thee, take another to help me make thy life pass pleasantly. Choose a fair bride, that she may be a delight to thine eyes; a young and strong one, that she may live long to be thy slave."

So the Sheikh chose a young girl from the sandy plains of the *Beni-Mzab*, who had not yet seen the date-palms fourteen times in flower. Her lips had the colour of the scarlet pomegranate; her eyes the glitter of the *yatagans* when the blades flash in the sunlight.

Her name was *Meryem*.

IV.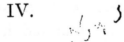

FROM the first moment Mansour beheld this fair star shining in the twilight of his father's tent, his heart was stirred; and when one day she let fall her face-cloth in his presence, he found her beauteous as one of the houris the Prophet promises to the elect of God.

He hastened from the tent in strong agitation, and wandered away he knew not whither. He was fain to hide his face from all men, lest the troublous thoughts that moved him should be legible in his eyes.

The following day he said to Kradidja, his mother:

" Mother, I must away from here."

" Wherefore, my son? You cannot quit your father's tent at the very time a new inmate has entered it. The wedding-rites are not yet ended, and you talk of leaving us? Would you anger your father, who will suppose you wish ill to the stranger? "

" Wish her ill? Who could imagine such a thing? Would to God, mother, you might find me so fair a bride."

' I will find you a fairer, my son! "

But he only shook his head.

Then she looked him in the eyes. He was her son, the son she loved and admired, in whom were centred all her joy and mother's pride. For him she was weakly indulgent, as mothers are.

More than once already she had heard reports of Mansour's ill-doings, at the hour when the women visit the fountain and repeat amongst themselves secrets that husbands must not know. She would listen to the tales, and grievances, and smile to herself.

In her mother's selfishness, she thought:

" Pray God, no harm touch the lad; for others, 'tis their own affair. Heaven is over us all; but each must guard his own."

No word of reproof was ever uttered to the son, no word of warning to the father of his son's evil courses.

But *now* she was afraid, and taking the boy's

head fondly between her hands, she drew his lips
down to hers:

"My child! I understand. Yes! you must from
home. Go, dwell beneath the tent of my brother,
the Caïd Abdallah. Enrol yourself one of the horse-
men of his *Goum* (Company); and if God so will,
you shall return to us with a fair wife. This very
day will I speak to Ahmet; meanwhile be watchful,—
watch your acts, nay! watch your very looks. The
prophet says, "Take not to wife such as have
been your brothers' brides,—it is a vile thing." But
the Prophet nowhere speaks of him who should
steal his *father's* bride; who could conceive an
outrage so abominable!"

Mansour, trembling and confused, would have
defended himself; but Kradidja put a finger on his
lips, and repeated the word, "An outrage!"

V.

HOWEVER when Kradidja spoke of sending him
away, the Sheikh replied he could not consent just
then to part with his eldest son. He needed him to
guard his flocks, and above all he required his help at
the approaching harvest! She dared not press the
point, and Mansour remained an inmate of the tent.

On learning the Sheikh's decision, he could not
check the flash of exultation that glittered in his eyes.

"Beware, headstrong boy!", his mother said
to him.

"Beware of what? In all the tribes of all the Souf there is no woman more fond and foolish than you, my mother! What is it you fear? And *supposing* your fear well-founded, would Meryem, think you, ever yield her consent?"

"A woman is like the reed that grows by the fountain-side," Kradidja replied; "she bends at the will of him in whose hands she is."

"But she is not in mine; she is my father's bride."

"A woman has but one heart, and her heart is his, who has the wit to win it... Enough, my child! but beware!"

Far from terrifying him, her words seemed but to encourage Mansour. Many a time a mother's weak complaisance is the direct cause of a son's vicious follies.

Be this as it may,—one morning when the Sheikh had left the tent, Mansour slipped noiselessly within, and hiding behind the *hamals* (sacks) of corn that held the year's supplies for man and beast, lay there silent and motionless, pretending to be asleep. But he was watching Meryem through the openings between the sacks; soon growing bolder, he would raise with one finger the border of the striped *tag* or curtain that divides the Arab's house of skins into two apartments, and himself invisible, saw every detail of the new-wed bride's toilette.

Her skin was olive-hued, with golden gleams where the light was reflected from the lustrous surface; and her rich dark hair fell in thick wavy masses below her waist, so that his gaze was lost in its depths. His thoughts tossed to and fro in a very tempest of longing, while the heady odours characteristic of brunettes mingled with the scent of rose and musk, and made his brain dizzy. He felt his strength going from him, and knew he could resist no more. Then he would rise noiselessly, run to where his flock fed on the plain,— seeming still to breathe from afar the intoxicating odours, his soul a prisoner in the meshes that had entangled his eyes.

VI.

HE ceased to lie in wait for the women, when they went to gather the dry branches of the broom and the *chichh* for fuel, or to fetch the supply of water for the household in the black goat-skins; and was no longer to be seen, as of old, guiding his flock to the river-side at the hour when half naked they perform *the great ablution.*

Then the young girls would blush and whisper amongst themselves, when suddenly they espied the burning eyes of the Sheikh's son peeping from some clump of oleanders.

Some feigning not to see him, quietly continued their bath, others more modest, would leave the water hurriedly and let down their *gandourah* (outer robe), terrified and covered with shame. But the older women would fall into a passion and cry shrilly:

"What are you looking at, child of the devil?"

"Not at you," he would reply. "You may bathe in security."

"Go to! go to! eternity were too short for you to wash out the stains of your abominations."

"Or you the marks of your uncomeliness, old hags! Quick! Cover up your ugliness; it makes me shudder!"

"*You* will be old some day; then the young will loathe you, and spit on your beard."

"Is it because the young loathe you, that *you* spit your venom at them?"

At this they would foam with rage and spit at him in scorn, and pursue him with curses, as he retreated, still taunting them as he went:

"Son of a dog! accursed Jew! you shall be the laughing stock of your wives once and again, and they shall heap mountains of shame upon your head! A scorn to every true believer, may you never pass the *Sirak*.* May you roll down, down from depth to depth of hell! Jew! cuckold! huckster! dog!"

At other times, hid in the thickets of juniper, he used to watch for the young girls to pass by. Then when they were so near he could see their light robes stirred by the evening breeze, he would call them softly by name:

* The narrow bridge over the abyss, which every Believer must cross to reach Paradise.

"Ho! Fathma, I love thee!"

"Embarka, I die of love!"

"Yamina, I am thine."

" Mabrouka, I would give my life for a look."

And so on to them all; for he loved them all, as boys do who feel the first down of manhood mantling on their cheeks.

VII.

BUT now the maids of the Ouled-Ascars met him no more in their path. No more did they feel his burning eyes fixed on them, eyes that seemed to look through and through them and follow them everywhere; no more did they hear those ardent declarations they loved to make a jest of, nor the furious abuse of the older women that made them laugh.

And folk said to Kradidja: " Tell us, Kradidja! Has the spirit of order breathed a good word in thy son's ear? or is he in love?"

His mother knew too well what passion held him in its grip, but she dared not say. To gratify her son, she would have sacrificed everything, the maidens of the tribe, the honour of families, Meryem —her husband's bride, Ahmet himself.

However she essayed yet another attempt.

" O Sheikh!" she said to Ahmet, one night that he came to visit her and lie in her couch,—for propriety requires a husband to give equally to

each of his wives the share of his favours due to
her, and it is written: 'He that has two wives,
and inclines to the one rather to the other, that man
shall appear at the Judgment on the Last Day
with buttocks one bigger than the other.' "O
my husband! I demand nought! I waive my rights.
Thou art my lord and master; but keep thy vigour
for Meryem, for I know well what the Prophet
says:

"'Thou mayest give good hope to whichsoever
wife thou wilt, and take to thy bed whichsoever
thou preferrest,—even her whom thou hast afore-
time slighted, but now thou desirest after her anew.
Let them never be aggrieved at what thou doest;
but let each be well content with that thou givest
her.'

"I am well content with thy good will. What
charm can my faded beauty have for thee after the
intoxication of Meryem's youthful loveliness. I am
not jealous; I have had my share, and it was the
best, for I enjoyed thy youth and the fulness of
thy manly vigour. But hearken to the advice of
thy first and fondest wife. Send away thy son
from home. In the peaceful plains of the Ouled-
Ascars young men fall asleep in sloth. Despatch '
him to the land of the Ksour; let him join the house-
hold of the Caïd of the Nememchas, to be trained
in the learning of the *Tolbas*,* or to be enrolled in
the ranks of his *mokalis* (warriors). Here he but

* Learned Men, Scholars; pl. of *Thaleb.*

wastes his time in dalliance with the maids, and presently will bring down some evil scandal on our name."

The Sheikh pondered a while before he answered:

"Kradidja, beloved! who wert the fountain of refreshment of my youth, and art now the stay and resting-place of my head, knowest not that all young men are so? It is the mother's task to safeguard her daughters, not the father's to watch his sons. But since thou art so fain the boy should leave us, perhaps it is really for his good. Later, when the harvest is gathered in, we will speak of the matter further. Come, beloved! the new bride cannot make me forget the old and faithful wife."

"Alas me!" thought Kradidja, "'tis to hinder his gathering the harvest of *thy* field, that I longed to see the child gone. Well! be it as thou wilt."

But she dared not give utterance to her thoughts, dreading to bring down his father's curse on the head of the son she loved so fondly.

VIII.

OLD husbands are suspicious, and a cruel jealousy pricks them night and day. There is a *djin,* a mischievous, mocking spirit, that loves to torment the guilty man; for he *is* guilty, who nips with the frost of his wintry years the sweet buds of springtime.

The Sheikh was already hastening fast towards his fortieth year when the child he was to wed had but just been born. He watched and guarded her, like the miser who has heaped a pile of *doüros* (dollars) in a *fondouk* (strong box). Day and night his vigilance never relaxes, and he dies with the words on his lips, " No robber shall have my gold!" Then some stranger, his heir, kicks his dead body on one side, forces the strong-box, and squanders the hoard.

He could not keep her sewn in a sack, nor tied to his *burnouse*, but his eyes were ever on the alert. Meryem never went to the fountain with the other women, nor to the plains to tear up the withered stalks of the hardy desert-grasses and break off the dead boughs of broom for fuel. At earliest dawn she would be turning the mill-stone that grinds the wheat for the day's use, always careful to raise a corner of the tent; so that her husband might see her. The latter stretched half-awake, half-asleep, on the soft fleeces of the bed she had just quitted, followed with his eyes the slow, graceful movements of the young wife, whose slender figure stood out in brilliant relief in the clear light of early morning. Soothed by the gracious sight and lulled by the monotonous grinding of the mill, he would sink into a happy lethargy of false security.

Soon the *douar* awoke, full day was come, and Meryem busied herself with the household cares of the tent. This was her allotted task, one the women always leave by common consent to the new wife, that the husband may have full enjoyment of her society. Perhaps too they think, "familiarity breeds contempt", and he will thus the sooner grow weary of her.

There he would remain, seated motionless and silent near the tent, his eyes gazing into space, letting the hours slip by in calm enjoyment of the happiness of the moment.

IX.

IT was seldom Mansour could find an instant when he could be alone with her; but there *were* such moments now and again. His father felt no distrust where he was concerned; and actually one day when obliged to leave the tent at a time at which all the women were away, he called him in and said, "Come, keep Meryem company."

Mansour sat silent, striving to hide his agitation. He dared not speak or even raise his head, for fear she should observe his emotion and read the longing he felt, in his eyes. When the Sheikh at length returned, she exclaimed. "Your son is timid as a girl!"

Kradidja reported her words to him, and rallied him on his supposed shyness. This made him desperate, and one evening as he was bringing home his flock, and Meryem came forward a few steps to meet him in pursuit of a she-goat that was wild and refused to obey her call, he threw a blossom into her bosom.

She plucked it out, laughing, and fastened it in her hair.

Next day he said to her:

"I long for a wife like you, Meryem. Tell me where to find one."

"Go," she answered, "go to the land of the Beni-Mzab, as your father did. You will find one there."

"Have the maids of the Beni-Mzab long hair as soft as silk like you, and eyes that sparkle so?"

"Yes! all this they have,—and more."

"O Meryem! every gesture you make scatters a keen perfume that burns my senses like a flame!"

"Hush, boy!—for you are but a boy. Your father is coming."

She called him a boy, though he was two full years older than herself; but she was fain to stay his too ardent words,—and indeed a younger sister is already a woman when her brothers are still only children.

He blushed and fell silent; but that evening he said to the Sheikh, "Father! to-morrow is the day of the great fair of the Beni-Mzab; I should love to go and see it."

"Well then, go! but do not tarry long from home."

He stayed away for more than a week, and said on his return that Meryem's father had kept him as his guest.

Meryem smiled, and as soon as they were alone, asked him:

" And when is the wedding to be, son of Ahmet? "

" Wedding? I shall never wed," he cried.

" What! could you find no fair girls amongst all the women of my tribe? are you so hard to please that none of my countrywomen satisfied you? yet I know some that are light and graceful as the gazelle, and their eyes as large and soft as the white cow's that gives us so much milk. "

" It may be so," he said, " I never looked at them. Yes! some maids I saw that half withdrew their veil from their faces to pleasure me, but my thoughts went not with my eyes. I sat under your father's tent; I wandered over the plains where you were born; I lay beneath the laurels by the river-side where you went to play as a child; I traced the outlines of the hills on the horizon that your eye first rested on when you awoke at dawn; I gazed long at all these things, and lo! I am returned. "

She pretended not to understand, and with a shrug of the shoulders, " Mansour-ben-Ahmet is surely mad. "

But only too well she knew what his madness was, and kept ever on her guard. Yet the young man's words pleased her; come whence it may, flattery is sweet in the ears of a woman.

It may be too that in her secret heart she thought she would have slept softer cradled in his lusty arms than with her white-haired husband.

" Why cannot we be suffered to choose as our heart dictates? are we bound to take from our father's hand the man he chooses to buy us?"

The complaint was a just one; and it is a just subject of reproach against us. Amongst the Roumis, your countrymen, is it not the same,—or worse? We buy a woman for her own worth, you value her for the dowry she brings.

This is why there are so many ill-assorted marriages in the world,—among believers and unbelievers alike. The young should mate with the young; such is the Law.

The greybeard who buys a young wife, does an abomination.

The father and mother who sell their daughter's maidenhood to a husband stricken in years, do an abomination.

What matter that the *cadi* (judge) or the priest have blessed the union. It is a prostitution none the less. The words he reads from his book over the heads of the bridal pair cannot wipe out the stain of the shameful bargain.

The man does an abomination who sanctions such a scandalous traffic in human flesh. The richer the old bridegroom is, the more guests come as witnesses to the marriage-feast, the more public the act of prostitution, the more abominable the crime.

And if the young bride, legally handed over to gratify the passion of a greybeard lover, sickens of his odious caresses and takes a disgust to husband and to marriage alike, she deserves the pity of all good men. She has been bought and sold; and the loathing she feels now at the dishonouring touch of her lord and master, is at once the cause and the excuse of the vicious follies she is bound to commit at a later time.

So is it written, or to this effect, in the book of our Lord Ali the Sublime, the husband of Fathma, Gateway of Knowledge and Lion of God, who says in the chapter that is called the *Kouffa*: "Ho! all true believers, repeat often the name of Allah, yea! celebrate his name morning and evening."

X.

BUT now he had once dared to speak, his reckless love burst all bounds, and welling from his heart overflowed his lips again and again.

"Meryem!" he said, "if you had to choose between my father and me, which would you have rather?"

She answered blushing, but showing no signs of anger:

"Hush! son of Ahmet, it is not becoming to speak so."

He said no more, obedient to her words, or perhaps afraid; and Meryem, surprised that she felt no annoyance at such audacious speeches, resolved for the future to avoid the dangerous proximity, and never to be alone with him. But at the same

time her eyes gazing over the far-away stretches of
the plain, she stood silent and pensive,—blind and
deaf to all else but one thought, that had possessed
her whole soul for days, " Oh! why did not the son
come first to ask my hand in place of the father? "

Why indeed? Fate only could have told the
answer. The course of many lives would have
been different. Weak man wanders at random in
the sea of the unknown; and each passing minute
may make the compass-needle of his destiny swerve.

If the son of Ahmet had gone first to the land
of the Beni-Mzab, and taken the fair Meryem to
his bed, the vast solitudes of Djenarah would not
after thirty years have re-echoed the cry of despair
you heard in the darkness:

" Afsia! Afsia! Afsia! "

XI.

MEANTIME the young larks were fluttering in
noisy, merry flocks in the ripening corn, the air
was laden with warm scents, everywhere man and
maid felt the languorous breath of summer in their
blood.

This was the time Kradidja dreaded; it is the
happy season of stolen kisses and stealthy meetings
amongst the waving yellow corn that clothes the
plain. As soon as the young shoots begin to
sprout and hide the brown earth, lovers' eyes meet,
and they sigh and say: " Summer will soon be

here!" Then the ripe corn-fields will make fine hiding-places. Starting from opposite points, lovers can glide along the furrows, slip between the stalks, to meet at last at the trysting-place, amid the waving golden grain.

Oh! the kisses,—stolen and found again, given and given back!

The blue sky looks down on them laughing; life, gay and abundant, murmurs, and sings, and whistles, and chirps, all round them; sudden shivers run along the standing corn; corn-flowers and poppies spread their petals, while the twittering nestlings, for a moment scared at the first fierce embraces, grow bolder and gaily sing their loves:

Oh! merry time,
When lovers meet
Among the wheat,
In summer's prime!

The goodman's fain
To catch the knave;
Nought can he save,
Nought but his grain.

Nought can he find;
The treasure's gone,
Help there is none;
Both eyes are blind!

Oh! merry lay,
The lark's fresh song;
The wheat among
Two lovers stray.

With bated breath
They whisper low;
Nought doth he know,
Both ears are deaf!

Wheat harvest's nigh;
Oh! the glad year,
Oh! the ripe ear,·
The blue, blue sky!

Oh! merry time,
When lovers meet
Among the wheat,
In summer's prime!

And when the harvester comes by to-morrow, he will lift the trampled corn with the point of his sickle, with a laugh or a curse, according as he is a young man or an old, —never dreaming that may be here his own honour has been trampled in the earth, never to rise again.

XII.

So the young larks disported themselves in the corn-fields, and Kradidja grew every day more and more anxious. She kept her suspicions secret, however; it was not for her husband she feared so much as for her son.

The latter never left the douar now. He was to be seen all day wandering near the tents, and became the focus of all eyes. Already men whispered together, and would soon be talking openly.

She took Mansour on one side, and making sure no one was within hearing:

"My son," she said, "beloved, too fondly beloved fruit of my womb! I beseech you, stay the calamity that threatens to overwhelm you, and me, and all of us. Go back again to the river-side as of old; lie hid, as you used, among the broom, waiting for the girls to pass by. Let them all see you there, all hear your words of love. What! is there not one of them all you care to choose? There are fair maids and gentle that blush at sight of you... Why long for the only fruit forbidden you, when you can pick and choose from so dainty a garden of girls? Hear your mother's words, Mansour! Two men there are walking in darkness,—that cannot see what passes round them, or hear what is said of them,—Ahmed and the son of Ahmed. Ah me! The young are headstrong, the old unheeding! and love is very strong!"

Kradidja wept; and her tears made the young man thoughtful and afraid. To put scandal off the scent, he went back to his old follies. Once again he lay in wait for the young girls at the river-side, and made fierce love to them.

They laughed merrily once more, and once more the old women cried:

"Oh! the villain! here he is back again! Ha! ha! the fruit your lips watered for was out of reach, was it? What an ado! Why, of course your vile flesh must be gratified! Bah! 'tis but food for worms!"

On her side Kradidja redoubled her vigilance, and kept repeating to the Sheikh, "Never leave Meryem alone!"

And when he expressed surprise at her advice, she added:

"Solitude is no safe companion for young heads. When a young wife is alone, Satan comes and tempts her, and is fain to make her trip. Watch her, my lord! Meryem is but a child."

XIII.

SUCH was the state of things when one morning two horsemen of the Nememchas arrived. They had ridden hard all night, for the news they brought was of the gravest.

The Sheikh and the men of the douar went out to meet them, to bid them welcome and lead them to the guest-tent.

Meanwhile the women had got ready the dardiaf (guest-tent), and spread the large carpets of thick soft wool. The corners of the tent were raised and secured to the tent-pegs, so as to establish through currents of air and keep the interior cool; and great jars or alcarasas of earthenware containing fresh water were suspended by cords of camel's hair, gladdening the eyes of the thirsty travellers.

They stretched their limbs in the shade, and as soon as they had quenched their thirst with water and with the milk their hosts offered in the

scttlas (jars) of lacquered iron, and had tasted the
cakes of dates and 'barley-meal served whilst the
couscous (mess of flour boiled in milk) was cooking,
the men of the tribe took their seats in a circle
round them, and the strangers spoke.

Bad news; and a chorus of exclamations of dismay.
The Caïd Hasseim, brother-in-law of Ahmed-ben-
Rahan, sent to warn him of the approach of the
dreaded Roumis. They were encamped already on
the plains of the *Meskiana*, and in such numbers,
the messengers declared, that a grain of barlay
could not have fallen from the sky without striking
an enemy's head, whilst their tents whitened the
desert like snow in bad winters.

It was fate at its darkest hour!

"What ill have we done the Roumis?" cried the
Sheikh; "what is it they want of us? we are men
of peace; we ask nothing save to live in quietness
with our flocks and herds. We owe nothing to
any man; we claim nothing of any. The men of
the Souf who have for ten seasons driven our flocks
to the North, can still remember the day when first
they heard the name of Roumis. Till then we
knew not that Franks dwelt beyond the blue sea;
yet now these same Franks are set up as masters
of the soil of our fathers! They ravage our har-
vests, spoil our flocks and herds, burn down our
palm-trees, and destroy our villages,—because for-
sooth Turks of Algiers we know nought of, twenty
years ago, attacked their ships, as they allege.

What is it they seek? Their own land, men say, is rich and fertile, their plains bear wheat and barley in abundance, they have noble gardens and many wealthy cities. But we are poor men; we have nought but the wide bare desert to call our own. What is it they hope to find in our sandy wastes? Silver? Nay! we have but little; yet, to save our lives, we will send them our scanty hoard, for they are mightier than we. Only let them leave us in peace!"

"And the men of your tribe, do they think as you do?"

"Yes!" replied the Sheikh; "but if any think otherwise, then let him speak."

But all held their peace.

Then, wrathful and indignant, the horsemen of Hassein cried:

"Cowards! are these your thoughts? Are these fit words for the sons of Islam? Is it in vain our lord, the Caïd, counted on you for help? He said, 'The *Ouled-Sidi-Abid* are men;' what will he say, when we tell him your reply, that we blush ever to have heard spoken!

"Even now the tribes of the northern Tell are on foot. Will you only stay behind in slothful ease with your women? Will you only be left solitary in your shame, the scorn of all brave men! O Sheikh! you cannot be one of those who say:

'The plague is come to our land;
Allah! let it spare my tribe!
The plague is come to our tribe;
Allah! let it spare my douar!
The plague is come to our douar;
Allah! let it spare my tent!
The plague is come to our tent;
Allah! let it spare my head!'

"Silver for the Roumis! of a surety God has left you to your own devices; and they are wicked and foolish. The sole metal they must win of us is *lead*."

"Yes! lead, lead!" the word was caught up by many voices.

"And your wives? Have you thought of them? What will they say when the warriors of the tribes of the Tell inscribe your name on the list of waverers and cowards?"

"We will march with you," cried the young men.

But their elders pondered, and shook their heads.

The discussion lasted long; and the Sheikh listened full of gloomy forebodings, and gave his opinion with a grave face and serious voice,—and forgot the very existence of fair Meryem.

XIV.

MIDDAY,—the hour when the steed treads his own shadow. Not a cloud floats in the liquid blue, not a breath bends the heads of barley and wheat in the ripening fields. The blanched stalks of the alpha-grass writhe under the intense heat of the sun's rays, while here and there the parched earth opens in cracks.

The hour of deepest stillness; the lark falls silent, the partridge sits motionless under the daffodils, the brown hare is fast asleep in the furrow. Only the harsh, shrill note of the cicadas is heard in the scorched grass, and the snap of the juniper seeds bursting in the heat.

The women have gone to fill the water-skins at the brook, and now seated on its banks under the shade of the laurels, they wait for the first breath of the evening breeze before returning.

Children, old women and dogs are all asleep in the tents, overpowered by the heat, and but for the men assembled in the *dar-diaf* the douar seems deserted.

At this hour, Mansour, leaving his flock to the charge of his young brothers, returned to the village in haste. He had seen from a distance the arrival of the horsemen, and was eager to know the news they brought.

Or perchance this was not the real motive urging him, but the wish to be near Meryem at a time when he knew his father could not but be occupied. Love had grown fiercer and fiercer in his untamed heart; and now nothing could assuage his desires but their fulfilment, nothing cure his longing but flight. But he could not fly; instead he hurried to find her, reckless and agitated. He had noted that

Meryem avoided him, and the fresh obstacle but
roused his passions further. Doubtless he did not
realize the enormity of such an intrigue, the foul-
ness of the crime he contemplated. He thought
not of consequences; his one idea was to be near
her, to feed his eyes on her beauty, to feast on
her smile, to gaze at the grace of her slender form
and the beauty of her limbs beneath the light robe
that fluttered in the wind.

I judge him not; I but report what befell, and
say:

"Love is very strong, very strong!"

XV.

HE glided through the high stalks of the ripe
barley, making a furrow through the grain, till he
was in front of his father's tent. There, stretched
full length on the hot ground, he fixed his burning
eyes on Meryem, following each slow languorous
movement of her form. In the half-light, beneath
the *haik* (veil) of white silk, she seemed to him to be
clad in a robe of sunshine. Presently she threw
herself on the cool mat of woven alpha-grass, and
he could vaguely distinguish, only half hidden
beneath the thin gauze, the lovely curves of her
shape, burning in the sun and seeming more than
ever beautiful to his excited senses.

The hard, sun-warmed surface of mother-earth
touched his bosom with a rough caress, while the

rays of the sun, father of all living things, blazed
down on his fevered head like flames of fire. Red-
hot sparks quivered in the overheated air, and
myriads of insects moved swiftly and silently in
the grass. The very stones he touched scorched
his limbs. Sudden starts and sighs seemed to fill
the air around him. The wanton earth laid bare
her bosom to the fertilizing embraces of the sun.

His senses were on fire. Suddenly he rose to
his feet; then, after hesitating for a few seconds,
his long shepherd's staff in his hand, he moved
towards the tent.

At the noise, slight as it was, his footsteps made
on the dry soil, Meryem raised her head quickly,
and gathering her *haïks* with all haste about her
over the gauzy mosquito robe that was her only
covering, cried angrily:

" What do you here? I tell you, begone! "

" Why are you angry, Meryem? " he said, hu-
miliated at his reception. " I am thirsty, and I
was coming to crave a *settla* of sour milk."

" There is no milk; begone! "

He looked at her shoulders, her arms, her neck,
and a fierce longing filled him to feast his lips on
them; but her flashing eye held him back, and he
left her, making for the guest-tent.

The men were still there, discussing the terrible
question that had suddenly sprung up like a nightmare
to disturb the quiet of their peaceable existence.

The edges of the great tent were raised breast-high all round, so as to let the air blow in freely on all sides, and to give each man his share of shade. Many however were left in the sun outside. The sweat rolled from their bronzed foreheads, trickling down the deeply lined cheeks on to their jet-black, square cut beards. But none felt heat or thirst; so absorbed were all by the peril that threatened.

Mansour approached the group silently, and sat down on his heels within hearing of the speakers.

XVI.

THE Sheikh Ahmed-ben-Rahan felt himself deeply aggrieved. The news of coming war was doubly hateful to him; he was a man of peace by nature, and he was but newly-wed. Not that he was a coward; like all the sons of Islam a warm and valiant blood coursed in his veins. But age had chilled his early enthusiasm. Besides no man cares, when he is running the risks of battle, to be exposed to other risks,—that threaten old men with young wives. War is like love; it is for the young. To be a father and a good soldier at one and the same time is hard. When the critical moment comes, the thought of children and wife *will* obtrude itself, and paralyses the bravest arm. Men that subordinate family to country are a small minority; the majority, and it is the majority that tells on the field of battle, think, though they do not say,—Family first, country second!

The Sheikh moreover had just heard other words that angered him. They were counting the number of horsemen the tribe could furnish, and Ahmed had just mentioned the name of his son. But one of the old men of the douar exclaimed scornfully:

"Oh! for him, best not count him! His proper place is tied to our daughters' skirts."

The father, furious at the insulting speech, had demanded what was meant; then all had answered with one accord:

"He speaks truth, Sheikh! What! are you the last to know of your eldest son's ill courses?"

And in the midst of listening to the complaints of fathers and husbands, the Sheikh perceived Mansour.

"What do you here?" he cried. "How comes it you are not at the river-side, watching the women? I have but now heard shameful tales of you. All men accuse you; and now you are here, you shall receive your chastisement publicly before all."

"Chastisement!" the young man repeated the word incredulously.

"Yes! chastisement, that I shall give you with my stick,—while I think of some punishment fitter for your conduct. Take heed! know you not your head is shaking on your shoulders?"

"Not it!" returned Mansour with a laugh, eager to cover the affront with a jest. "My head sticks firm on my neck, and will want a *flissa* (long knife) wielded by a strong hand to loosen it."

But not one of the group echoed his laugh, while

the envoys of the Caïd Hassein looked at him coldly and sternly.

"There are strong hands among the *Sidi-Abid*," said a grave voice.

"There are," added another voice, "and some day one of us will go to see Ahmed-ben-Rahan and will say: 'Sheikh Ahmed, I am your friend, and I esteem you, but your son Mansour has insulted my sister, my daughter; and, lo! I have killed him. See! yonder the village dogs lick the blood that flows from his neck.' And Ahmed-ben-Rahan will have to bend to the blow, and say: 'You have done well. The law is just; what is written must be fulfilled!'"

"Of a surety, I will say so; I swear it by the tomb of the Prophet! But enough said of such matters; they sound but ill in the ears of a father. For you, hearken! The Roumis draw near. As they advance, they destroy all before them like a cloud of locusts. They have burned the villages and the crops of the Tell, and destroyed the olives and pomegranates and vines; now they, are cutting down the palm-trees, those good gifts of God,—the palms that need the heat of twenty summers before they fruit. The messengers here declare the plain of the Meskiana is covered with their tents as thick as the firmament with stars, that wherever the eye falls, nothing is to be seen but the blue cloaks of the Franks. The tribes of the Tell appeal to us of the Beled-el-Djerid to unite with them to drive out the Unbelievers. But when the young men mount and ride against the foe, you must stay at the tent-door with the little children and watch them go. Yes! all proclaim you unworthy to hear the sound of arms, you that love only to hear women's loose talk. In this matter are sure signs for such as reflect, and already the men of the Sidi-Abid begin to say, when they see you: '*He* will never be a warrior to ride with us in days of danger.' "

"They lie," cried the young man, trembling with passion. "They lie, and I will show them they lie!"

But no one heeded the boast, and a smile hovered over the lips of many.

"You talk like a new-made wife, that boasts and tells her companions, 'I am the fairest of you all;' but it wants more than fine words to make folk fair,—or brave. It wants deeds to prove what you can do, and your deeds heretofore have been those of a slave to fleshly lusts. Even as the daughters of Fathma, the handmaidens of sin, you shall be treated like them. Why shave your head? Nay! let your locks grow long. I will give you circlets of silver for your arms and ankles, ear-rings for your ears. Meanwhile, go take a pitcher; away to the fountain to join your sisters."

"Sheikh," exclaimed Mansour, boiling with rage and shame, "one day I shall know how to prove you wrong in reckoning me among the women; I will prove you all mistaken. Not another night will I sleep in this douar where the men reject me from their *goum*. On your heads, on all your heads, be it; you shall repent of your words, you shall repent of them and wish they had never been spoken, the day you come to kiss my stirrup and call me lord."

There was a shout of laughter, but he continued:

"Sheikh! give me a horse and a musket, and I will go join the Caïd Hassein. He will welcome me in his *goum*, and as you have rejected me, henceforth I will serve under him. By the tomb of the Prophet, from to-day you may blot out my name from among the Sidi-Abid .... Warriors of the Nememchas, I will follow you whither you go. They will still be deliberating what they have to do next, when young and old in this land shall hear tell of Mansour-ben-Ahmed's prowess in the war."

All laughed again mockingly, and one of the old men said softly:

"The lion's skin on the ass's back!"

Another• said. "He has a tongue of gold, like a Thaleb. From henceforth we agree to call you Sidi. Lo! Sidi-Thaleb-Mansour-ben-Ahmed, I am your servant!"

"Good!" added the Sheikh; "but the Tolbas* are but curs in war. The noise they make hinders them from doing much. They bark, but they never bite."

"*I* mean to bite," said the young man.

"My son, I see fury in your eyes, and I hear furious words from your lips. Your anger pleases me; he who feels an insult bitterly, will learn how

¹ Plural of Thaleb.

to avenge it. I know your demand, and I give
my consent. Your mother has long been urging it.
You may yet distance our young warriors in the
race. You will confirm by word of mouth what
we have just delivered to the envoys of Hassein,
'So soon as he shall ask its aid, he shall have
our *goum*.' Go, saddle the black colt. He was
the first foal of my good mare *Haama*, and may
you one day say: 'he has carried me well and faith-
fully.' When you return from the battle-field, the
wife you have chosen shall take his head between
her arms, and unfasten her *haïk* to wipe the foam
from his lips. Go, and my blessing go with thee!"

And as he was retiring, the Sheikh called after him:

"Bid Meryem open the *fondouk*, and give you
two douros and five and twenty cartridges. For
the rest, God will provide."

XVII.

MANSOUR'S retreat was followed by a burst of
merriment. The men of the douar were saying to
one another: "Ha! ha! the Roumis will fly when
they see him!"

He looked back, and a smile was on his father's
face. The sight cut him to the heart, and made
his fury boil up once more, for he did not hear the
words his father added: "Have patience; the boy
is of a good stock, and when his beard is grown,
he will know well how to hold his own among
brave men."

Arrived at the entrance of the tent, he threw down his herdsman's staff, and it rolled to Meryem's feet.

"What! returned again?" she exclaimed. But then, terrified at the fierce light that burned darkly in his eyes, she drew back into the interior of the dwelling of skins, and leant against one of the tent-poles.

She had just completed her toilette, and her face was freshly painted. Her great dark eyes, that the *koheul* (black pigment) yet further magnified, were deep wells of love; and the lovely arched brows were prolonged at the extremities till they reached the temples, and united by a slender dark line. She had chewed the *souak*, that lends the lips the scarlet of the pomegranate-seed, and fixed on her cheeks tiny spangles of gold, that Mansour devoured with his eyes and burned to touch with his lips. The ample turban of the women of the Souf crowned the graceful head, framed in the heavy ringlets of its dark tresses, from which her great silver ear-rings peeped out with brilliant effect. The *gandourah* of striped silk was half open in front and allowed a glimpse of her small, firm breasts, that a husband's kisses and the fatigues of child-birth had had no time to wither. Her bosom rose and fell rhythmically beneath the light robe that was confined at the waist by a girdle of gold embroidery. Arms and limbs were bare. Her hands were stained yellow with *henna* to the wrists, her feet to the ankles; and the delicate nails of fingers and toes were like the berries of the jujube-tree.

It is written: "When a woman has made beautiful her eyes with *koheul* and her fingers with *henna*, and has chewed the branch of the *souak*, that perfumes the breath, making the teeth white and the lips of purple, then is she more pleasant in the sight of God, for that she is more loved of her husband."

And when she raised her arm to grasp the tentpole, against which she leant her head in an attitude of careless grace, Mansour's burning eyes fixed on the ravishing hollow of the armpit, from which the hair had been scrupulously removed, and on the harmonious curves of neck and bosom.

No! never before had he seen her so charming; never since her marriage day had her beauty so dazzled him.

And trembling with emotion, he stood speechless before this epic of loveliness.

XVIII.

MERYEM blushed under his gaze that was more eloquent than any words of love, and felt the delicious flattery of his admiration of her beauty.

"What, you! you returned again! Surely I bade you begone."

She strove to give her voice a tone of anger; but she could not. The sentence that began in wrathful tones died away softly into silence; and with more of surprise than of displeasure she saw

Mansour draw from his girdle a little ring of silver and seize her hand.

His look was so beseeching, she dared not refuse the gift. Covered with blushes, she let him put it on her finger, laughing to hide her agitation.

"Is this our betrothal?" she asked.

His only purpose had been to beg her keep the ring as a souvenir, and bid her farewell. Possibly too he had dreamt of snatching a kiss from her rosy mouth. In any case Meryem's laugh emboldened him, and he replied at once:

"Yes! it is our betrothal. Are you not decked out for the coming wedding?"

"Wedding! ah! it was over long ago. You know that. Your father has not divorced me yet, so how can I marry again?"

The words ended in a sigh, and Mansour sprang forward to catch it as it left her lips; but his courage failed him. He merely took possession of the little hand he had dropped after slipping the ring on her finger, and pressed it in both his own.

Then he sat down at the feet of his idol, and laying his forehead in the soft hand, began to weep.

Stirred with pity, she stooped and touched his shoulder:

"Why do you weep, Mansour?"

He made no answer, and she felt his tears trickle over her fingers.

"Why weep like a little child his mother scolds?

You are no more a child; I am not your mother, and I do not scold you. Up! Mansour. What would the Sheikh think, if he saw you so? What would Kradidja think, who is so suspicious? Mansour! Mansour! What would the men of the douar say?"

"What care I? Let me lie at your feet, I am happy there."

"Mansour! up! I beseech you."

"You ask what men would say," he returned. "Why! what could they say but what has been said many a time already, 'The son of Ahmed is dying for the love of the Rose of the *Ouled-Sidi-Abid!*'"

She withdrew her hand sharply, and gazed at him overwhelmed by his words.

"Tell me! have they seen that you loved me?"

"Yes!" he cried, embracing her limbs and kissing her feet madly, "I love you, love you; and you always knew it!"

"I do *not* know it, I *will* not know it. Up! up! Mansour. Are you mad?"

"Yes! I am mad; I must be mad, for I have done all I could to tear up the thought of you from my heart. I have rolled among the sharp prickles of the broom; I have spent long hours in tears hid in the oleander-thickets. But in spite of me, my lips kept murmuring all the time, 'Meryem! Meryem'. I strove to love the maids of the douar, but I could not. 'Twas you I loved, even when I

was whispering words of love in their ears; and
when I sighed, 'twas to you my sighs flew. Yes!
Meryem, yes! I am mad."

"Hush! child, hush!"

"Ever since the day you came, a guest thrice
blessed and thrice accursed, to dwell beneath my
father's tent, and I beheld you lift your veil and
show the dazzling loveliness of your face; ever since
the day the warriors of the tribe fired their merry
salute to welcome you, while you, you sat in thought
with pensive eyes, not hearing the crash of the
guns nor the neighing of the fiery steeds nor the
women's cries of joy, seeing nothing, when all saw
nought but you; ever since the horrid night I heard
you utter your first cries of pain, that my father's
kisses could not stifle,—I have indeed been mad!"

"You make me die of shame."

"Let me tell you all, Meryem! I counted them,
your cries, yes! every one. And when the other
women whispered low, and laughed among them-
selves, I was tearing my breast with my nails.
Look! you may yet see how often, for since that
time the dates of the oasis have but barely had
space to ripen."

He rose to his feet, and opening his *gandourah*
showed his chest torn with long red marks.

"Go! go! Have pity on me. I cannot, I must
not, listen to you longer. Go!"

She tried to escape, but he stood in front of her,
his arms wide open to seize her.

"My love! my life!" he cried; "I long for the sweets of your bosom, I long to drink there, I long to die there!"

XIX.

A FRENZY of passionate love had seized him, fierce and irresistible, that made him deaf to every appeal of conscience.

Women plead in his excuse,—he was so young and did not think. They throw the blame on Meryem, and say she was a coquette and weak. But there! women are the bitterest enemies of women; if the plain were empanelled as judges, they would condemn all the fair to death. Men, colder and more impartial critics, declare Mansour the guilty one. Thus human justice sees the same act in different lights; the Immutable alone can read the heart.

You of the North, you cannot understand these whirlwinds of fiery passion.

In your cold land love is a puny dwarf; it makes humble slaves of you, with bent head and downcast eyes. You flutter round women like foolish gaudy butterflies; you coo like doves, and mince your words as wantons do. Truly it is a question which are the more womanish, your women or your men. No wonder if the manly sons of the Prophet, seeing your young men, slim and all but beardless, with rouged faces and hair perfumed and curled, take them for girls, and would make love to them.

Your sun has no heat; your life knows no fatigue or danger. What wonder your love is thin and weak as water.

'Tis thus your women dare 'to display the allurements of gesture and of dress, of words and looks, they do. They fear not to expose their faces in public, and even to heighten the beauty of them for greater enticement; nay! in your *salons* they go farther and display their opulent shoulders, and the velvety hollow of the back between them that entices wanton thoughts to follow its downward curve, and bare their bosoms, by secret devices making them yet more prominent and seductive to the prying eye. And the charms they cannot show, these they complacently suggest by artful tricks of toilette, to better excite desire.

Desire? yes! but what are your desires worth?

Supposing, enticed by the beauties you have seen, or guessed, the charms they have shown you, or hinted at, you whisper in humble and adoring accents, "I love you, fair lady!"—why! they are insulted, and reply with scorn, "Sir! I have a husband." Then, like a child his mother threatens with the whip, you slink away ashamed.

But what is it all to me? Only I ask,—if you *have* a husband, woman, why does he make a show of you, like a tradesman with his wares to sell? Let him keep your nakedness and your fair flesh for himself alone. Satiated glutton, let him not tantalize hungry men with the exhibition of the rich fare he revels in.

Hide your treasure; 'tis the surest way not to have it stolen.

But, the fact is, among you Franks all this leads to little or nothing,— good or bad. You look and sigh,—and that is all! But it is very different with the sons of Arabia, whom the *Simoom* scorches with its breath of flame, and fires the blood.

I am not speaking of the *Chaouias* or the *Bedouis*, whose women may be seen by every stranger cultivating the fields of the Tell. They are beasts of burden, that work half-naked, exposing to public view their thin toil-worn shapes and dangling breasts like a she-goat's dugs. Such are not women, but mere creatures of misery that from infancy have been enslaved to heavy manual labour too hard for them, and as mere children fouled and brutalized by premature vice. But the fair daughters of the Souf are very different; and no man can look on them without peril. Pale or golden-olive in complexion, their great dark eyes are wells of love; and the young man of our race who is privileged by fate to catch a glimpse of one of these dazzling forms, cries, with an oath by the head of the Prophet: "Oh! to kiss her sweet mouth, and die!"

So did Mansour; and strove, his eyes flashing with the frenzy of desire, to grasp Meryem in his arms.

XX.

SHE pushed him back, confused and terrified by his vehemence. "What are you doing? Mansour, listen to reason. You are not in your senses. The old witches of the tribe have cast a spell over you. Do not hurt me! do not force me to cry for help! Consider,—the least sound will bring your father here, and everybody; and there will be a scandal that will ruin all. Remember whose wife I am. Mansour! Mansour!"

He saw at once force would be of no avail, and that he must resort to stratagem.

"Hear me, Meryem. It is my duty to tell you what I am going to reveal. The men you see yonder are horsemen sent by the Caïd Hasseim to summon the tribe to fight for our country. All are ready. But one of them said jeering the Sheikh, 'No! Ahmed-ben-Rahan is not ready. He has married a young wife, and he loves the perfume of her petticoats better the smell of powder.' My father protested indignantly; then the Sheikh of the Ouled-Rabah took up the word:

" 'By all I have been told, Ahmed, this flower of the Souf would bloom more luxuriantly at your son's lips than planted in your grey beard! Each is free to please himself; yet is it a pity when a young wife is tied to an old warrior's arm. She makes his blows feeble and uncertain, for the thought of her will be with him even on the battle-field."

" 'You speak truth,' replied my father, 'the devil tempted me that day I first longed to have her in my bed. She is but a child without a thought or care but to paint her eyebrows and stain her fingers and toes with *henna*. I had done better to have told my son, "Take her, you!"'"

"He said that?"

"By my head, did he! And the Sheikh of the Ouled-Rabah added, 'Yes! you are right. The young for the young!'"

"If he really said those words, I will ask a divorce; but you are lying, you know you are lying."

"I can prove what I say is true. I had been standing aloof, but at this I came forward."

"I saw you."

"And I said, 'Father, it is not yet too late; and if you are tired of your bride .... I am ready to take her.' Then they all laughed."

"How rash!" cried Meryem. "Yes! I heard them laugh."

"But my father answered, 'The Law forbids it.'"

"What! is that the only reason he gave against it?" the simple-minded girl asked.

"The only reason. Is it not sufficient? Oh! Meryem, Meryem, how could you endure the caresses of a man of his age without loathing? Cannot you see that the sheets of your bridal bed but make a death-cold shroud? But *I* am young like you.

Hear how wildly my heart beats, and taste how my lips burn with fire."

" A curse be on my head, if ever I commit a sin so grievous! A curse on your wicked head; you would stain the bed of the father that begot you!"

" Rose of Paradise! there *is* no stain, for my father himself repents that he ever married you."

" You lie, child of the devil. What you tell me is impossible. You are like the Christians, that juggle with words and distort their meaning of set purpose, making confusion worse confounded with their false tongues."

" I swear by the Prophet I speak truth. Shamed by the jeering speeches of the Sheikh of the Ouled-Rabah, my father said before them all,—I repeat word for word:

" 'Some day we will have a divorce; then I will give her to you for handmaid, even as King Solomon received from his father David's bed his handmaid Abisag.' "

" He could never have said that! It is a falsehood."

" How should I dare to lie, when you can convict me of the falsehood instantly?"

" I repeat, it is a falsehood."

" O! Meryem, you are more beautiful than the gazelle, but you are not gentle like it. You are obstinate, as the she-goat is obstinate; and will *not* believe the truth."

And without giving her time to think, he seized

her arm, and drawing her from the tent, called to the old Sheikh who was haranguing the assembled crowd.

"Sheikh! O, Sheikh! Ahmed-ben-Rahan."

"Well?" asked the old man, annoyed at the interruption.

"Meryem will not believe me. She says it is a falsehood I speak."

Then the Sheikh, furious at his young wife thus showing herself unveiled before strangers, cried in passionate tones:

"The boy speaks the truth. Hear him, I command you. And trouble me no more."

Humiliated at these rough words addressed to her in public, and still more at the yet greater insult she believed herself to have received, she sprang back into the tent, furious and amazed.

"Now you see," cried Mansour, "sooner or later you will be mine. Let it be sooner; let me have my rights now."

And he had kissed her neck and arms and lips madly, before she recovered self-possession.

"I will make complaint to the *Cadi*. Mansour, your father is a villain. Leave me, leave me."

"Yes! fair flower of the morning, he is a villain, and the curse fall on *his* head."

He glided to her feet, and drew her to the ground by his side.

"Oh! leave me," she kept repeating, "I will complain to the *Cadi!* I will complain to the *Cadi!*"

But her resistance grew weaker and weaker in proportion as her lover became more bold. Soon it ceased altogether, and Mansour heard only a last feeble protest that escaped the lips of the desperate girl, a low, murmured, "I will complain to the Cadi ...."

XXI.

THE outrage once accomplished, the evil was beyond remedy and complaints useless.

When Meryem discovered the trick that had helped to her undoing, she did not cry out or tear her hair. Neither did she say, "You have undone me! You are a villain!"

She knew herself to be as guilty as her incestuous lover, and putting a finger on her lip, looked Mansour in the face:

"All is over now. You must go, and never return. Your presence is a pollution. We must see each other no more. Swear, swear, you will not come back."

"I will never come back," he repeated after her.

"What faith can I put in your words? You have shown yourself a master of cunning lies."

But Mansour repeated simply: "I swear that I will never come back again."

Then she helped him to saddle the black colt.

In his interest no less than for her own sake, she wished him gone. Well she knew that, if he stayed, their first fault would not be the last. It would infallibly be followed by many another, till at long last punishment overtook the guilty pair.

For punishment always does overtake the guilty, and the slower its coming, the more terrible is it at the last.

When she saw him mount the black colt, she wept. But Kradidja, who more than once afterwards found her in tears, could not tell whether it was her sin she wept for, or the hurried departure of the lover that took her heart with him.

The horsemen of the Caïd Hasseim were waiting for him; and soon they made a start.

"Farewell!" said the Sheikh, "the blessing of God, and mine, go with you."

"Prosper, and come back soon," cried his comrades.

But he could not answer a word. Already he felt a remorse, that seemed to choke him, and made him dumb.

"Forgive him," said his father, "he is still indignant at the insult he received. But we shall hear great things of him yet; I know what blood is in his veins."

The rest smiled.

Meryem, standing at the threshold of the tent, gazed long after him, one hand pressed to her bosom and her face still red from his fierce kisses. She seemed no longer to feel her heart beat, and cried in anguish:

"My heart is bound to his, and has gone along

with him. And I made him swear never to come back again."

When now far away, to disappear in a moment behind the first swell of the plain, he drew rein, and turning round stood a moment motionless, illuminated by the dying fires of the setting sun.

Then the men of the *douar*, who had all risen to their feet, laughed and shouted to him:

" *Sidi-Thaleb ! Sidi-Thaleb !* we salute you."

But he neither saw them nor heard them. He did not even see his father who was wildly waving his *burnouse* in a last farewell, nor his mother who cried through her tears, " My son, may your belly never want bread ! ", nor the maidens of the *douar* who sent their good-wishes after him. All he saw was a silken *haïk* that a little hand shook from the door of his father's tent, and two tears coursed down his cheeks.

When he had disappeared from sight, the fair Meryem turned and looked on her husband, who still stood, his eyes fixed on the horizon, straining to catch another glimpse of his son's vanished form.

"Oh! may he never know," she murmured to herself, " the sin we have been guilty of ! May his days be spared that sorrow ! Yes! better that my darling never, never return ! "

XXII.

HE joined the ranks of the *goum*, and in the hour

of battle when the sabre is red with blood and eye meets eye in hate, he bore himself in such wise that the old warriors said to him after the fight, " Well done ! "

His valour raised the repute of his tribe. Men said, " He is brave; he is one of the *Ouled-Sidi-Abid !* " The old Sheikh Ahmed trembled with pride one day when he overheard the words, " Look! the father of Mansour the Brave."

But he never returned; nor was Meryem ever to see him more. She strove to forget, but in vain. Long she waited for him, and many a time she watched the plain, looking to East and West, North and South, and asking, " From what quarter will he come, and when? " And if she saw far away at the horizon a troop of horsemen appear, or a little cloud of dust rise, she would tremble through all her being, and cry, " 'Tis he ! "

" 'Tis he ! " the Sheikh would repeat, whose eyes also scanned the desert, and a tear of joy would trickle down his wrinkled cheek.

" 'Tis he ! " the aged Kradidja would repeat, and shake with excitement. "God has heard my prayer; I shall not die before I have seen once more the first and fairest fruit of my womb."

And men-servants and maid-servants, and the men of the *douar*, would look over the plain, and say, " 'Tis he ! "

But it never was. Weeks, months, years passed and neither Mansour nor the black colt came back again.

Once, however, all were sure they saw him; and
joy and excitement filled their hearts to over-
flowing. A horseman approached riding a steed
the whole *douar* knew for the foal of *Naama*, the
devourer of Space.

" It is he! it is! Kradidja! Meryem! Go, kill the
fattest sheep. It is my son!   Unroll the Tunis carpet,
and spread it on the floor. My children, I can die
in peace. It is Mansour! My son! O, my son! "

All the village was astir, shouting:

" Ho! young men! up, up! High day and holi-
day! A salvo of your muskets to welcome Mansour
the Brave! 'Tis Mansour-ben-Ahmed come back! "

They no more called him the *Thaleb* in mockery.
but all shouted in chorus:

" Mansour the Brave! Mansour the Brave! *Ma-
rhababek! Marhababek!* Welcome! thrice wel-
come ! "

Meryem turned pale and shuddered, as if the
fever of *El-Meridj* were in her veins; but Kradidja
shook her roughly and chid her:

" What! Meryem. Come, courage! Courage! or
your shame will be an open secret. You will betray
yourself."

But the horseman had stopped a gunshot away,
and sat there motionless.

He watched the preparations making in his honour,
but came no nearer.

Then the old Sheikh went forward to greet him,
followed by a group of the men of the tribe: but

when to his surprise he saw him still motionless in the same spot, and holding in his horse, that danced with impatience and saluted the tents of the *Ouled-Ascars* with joyous neighs, he waved his *burnouse* and cried in a loud voice:

"Come nearer! come nearer, Mansour!"

And he stretched his arms towards him, then pointed to his heart.

His companions also waved their *burnouses*, and shouted: "Mansour! Mansour! *Marhababek! Marhababek!*"

Of a sudden they saw the horseman raise his right arm.

Long he held it outstretched, pointing towards the *douar*; then putting his hand to his lips, he threw a kiss in the same direction, that seemed to carry his very soul with it.

It was Mansour's first greeting, and his last farewell, to his father's venerable countenance and white beard, to his mother who called his name, to a light brilliant form that stood beside her, to the great brown tent with its yellow stripes, that had seen his birth and had sheltered his slumbers for many a year, to the maidens he had made love to, now doubtless wives and mothers, to men, to women, to flocks and herds, to all. He cried:

"Greeting to you all! God's blessing is with you; lo! I will not bring down misfortune on your heads, for I am accursed! accursed!"

And filled with amazement they saw him wheel

his horse sharply round, spur him into a furious gallop, and disappear, without one backward glance, in a cloud of dust that glittered golden in the setting sun.

Mansour had been very near breaking his oath, but sudden remorse stayed him. He dared not sleep beneath the tent he had polluted, his father's tent, nor see once more the woman he had wronged; he dared not meet the calm eye of the father he had betrayed. This was his punishment. God punishes in such wise as seems good to God.

XXIII.

TIME slipped by without destroying the hope of his return. Now and again his name reached the *douar*, born by the din of battle; but that was all.

They were still waiting and watching for him, when one morning the *douar* was swept away, as by a whirlwind of the fierce *simoom*. At day-break, the hour when a man is unarmed, a horse unbridled and a woman ungirdled, the Roumis passed that way; and the sun was not yet high in the heavens when all was over and not a living thing left on the plain.

Of the *douar* and its seventy tents, of the flocks Mansour had guarded of old, of the fair Meryem and the haughty Kradidja, of the old Sheikh and the *Ouled-sidi-Abid* not a vestige remained,—only a memory of what *had* been.

At twilight came the marauders that prowl under cover of night, to rob the dead. They saw the corpses of women that the horsemen of the *Magzen* had violated and then ripped up. They had already been stripped of their silver circlets, their brace-lets and finger-rings. Such is war. If men risk their lives, they must have their reward. Soldiers must have their amusement when the fight is won.

Still a little silver ring had escaped their notice. It lay wrapped in the folds of an amulet over the heart of one of the dead women.

There was nothing else left to *loot* but a few blood-stained *burnouses*, a few tattered tents, a few torn *haïks*. These they carried off; and the jackals had the rest. The poor must live.

XXIV.

MANSOUR was ever in the thickest of the fight in every battle. He had his people to avenge, and his past to forget.

Death, who takes cowards by the throat, slinks away abashed before those who defy him. Gun to shoulder, and sword in hand, Mansour sought death. The Roumis could not count the victims of his blade; his ball, men say, never touched the ground.

But what cared he for glory? To forget was all he wished.

When we were at last vanquished by the supe-rior strength, numbers and discipline of the enemy,

and also, it must be owned, by the treachery of
our own people, like the rest he bent his head
before the storm.

What use to strive against fate? Fate is like a
raging mountain torrent that of a sudden sweeps
down from the heights. Wise men avoid its course;
it is only fools that try to bar its progress, and
their dead bodies soon go ·to swell the mass of
debris scattered over the plain. So he drew aside,
and avoided the fury of the storm.

But it is in perils that a strong man's soul is
tempered. The man who sits still at the doorway
of his tent, watching the hours go by, contented with
what God gives him, will never have Fame and
Fortune for companions.

They are women, and surrender only to the lover
who is bold and enterprising. Mansour found
both in the course of his· restless wanderings up
and down the highways of life in search of forget-
fulness.

He found them in the land of the Souf; he chased
them across the boundless solitudes of the desert,
and seized the intangible skirts of these *houris* that
men so long after.

He forced them to his will, there on the desert
road, beset with perils, that the caravans follow, the
caravans that cross the Sahara to the wild regions
beyond in search of buffalo-skins and gold-dust, and
ivory and handsome negro slave-women.

He had made himself a man of renown among

the brave; and he did the like again among rich merchants and bold traders.

Every enterprise succeeded with him, and he won the surname of *Sidi-Messaoud*, or "My Lord the Happy Man"; for among Believers alike and Unbelievers, the crowd worships success.

"The Happy Man!" He might have been happy, could he have forgotten the past!

He might well have been happy, for wiser than many rich men, whose first and only idea is to heap up *douros* upon *douros*, to accumulate a hoard and then never use it, he employed the reward so nobly won by his toil and intrepidity on his pleasures, those crumbs of happiness the Master throws us to reconcile us to life.

Then for a little while he would forget. Inexorable memory ceased for a while to torture him; the viper of remorse for a while was still. He was able to forget that he was accursed.

XXV.

RETURNING from those vast solitudes where a traveller may journey for months together and find no limit to the desert, he would often meet on the borders of the Souf caravans of the traders of the Sahara, who as summer approaches, halt in the northern plains to pasture their flocks and buy the corn of the Tell in barter for ostrich-feathers and dates from the oases. Then he would ask leave to

join his caravan to theirs; and weary of the monotony
of the long march, they would accept the offer with
delight, for he was well-known as a promoter of
hunting parties and merry doings.

Then would the firing of many guns break the
eternal silence of the desert, for *El-Messaoud* was
no niggard of powder; then the women from their
palanquins would strike their fingers on their mouths
and laugh and make the air throb again with loud,
shrill, *staccato* cries of joy, cries modulated in a
certain rhythmical melody that has power to stir
men's hearts and intoxicate the senses like the for-
bidden thing, wine; then the camels, tossing their
heads aloft, would stretch out their great tawny
necks eagerly, while flocks and herds in terror
would gallop away in front. Then the proud, strong-
chested stallions of the *Haymour* and the mares
with their ample loins, all trembling with excitement,
would dance and curvet over the sand.

Then salvo after salvo! Volley after volley in quick
succession. Horsemen dash wildly to and fro; the
long *chelils* (ornamental horse-cloths) of silk toss their
gold fringes in the wind; muskets are thrown high in
air, and caught again by nimble hands. Young men
and old, straining over their horses' manes, sweep off
at a tearing gallop, and disappear, pursued by the wild
shouts of the women in a yellow whirlwind of dust.

And far away on the golden levels of the plain
ostriches fly in terror, and troups of gazelles bound
out of sight.

" Fair land that Heaven loves,—a land of freedom, remote from Roumis and Sultans! Fair unknown land!"

XXVI.

BUT his chief pre-occupation was—Love. In this too he was a warrior of approved valour, and successful as became so intrepid a campaigner.

The black slave-girls of the Soudan had satiated him with the mad intoxication of their fierce caresses, and he would feel the craving to refresh his appetite on the fragrant bosoms of the fair daughters of the Souf,—the softest, sweetest pillow for a man's head that God has given.

Wonder of wonders! fair daughters of the Souf and the *Beled-el-Djerid*, whose eyes are wells of passion and have the bright gleam of yatagans! The sight of your beauty warms the blood like the outposts' camp-fire, when dawn is just breaking over the hills and the morning air is chill.

None better skilled than he, at the hour when the heavens are like molten brass, to watch for the timid daughters of Hagar, when as the caravan is on the march they peep out inquisitively by the *taka* (curtained opening) of their litter, and show them, unseen by every other eye gay kerchiefs striped with golden braid or necklaces of coral or circlets of silver of cunning workmanship or magic amulets,—the keys that like the *Sesamé* of our Arab tales unlock the gates bolted and barred by jealous husbands.

By the time evening was come, and the long-winding caravan was gliding silently through the blue haze, as the sun descended behind the swelling hills on the western horizon and shot broad rays of golden light across the sky, while the horsemen in front with musket on shoulder drove before them the tired flocks. peering into the distance to find the palms that mark the long-sought well, — Mansour had made his choice.

This is the moment when a bold lover may scale the red litter perched on the docile camel's back, hidden from the husband's eyes.

Then the fair maid of the Desert, trembling and exhaling the very perfume of love, would stretch her rounded arm to help him, her silver bracelets clashing together with a merry chime, and would shut close the yellow curtain, and welcome him to her breast.

Thus many a sweet hour was his,—of those hours that heaven is so niggardly in giving, and which fly by so swiftly they do not count in the lapse of time.

On long and tiresome journeys, when the sun dazzles and the sand scorches, amid the stifling dust raised by the camels' slow, heavy feet, amid dangers and weary watchings and burning thirst, he had wit to drain these drops of the refreshing dew of life that is called Love.

So would he win forgetfulness.

Time with its vicissitudes is in a strong man's

hands. He can do with it what he will, and, after God, is arbiter of his life.

XXVII.

MANY a time too on moonless nights when the dogs alone guarded the sleeping *douar*, he prowled, a dauntless thief that recked not of husbands' rights, round the tent containing the object of his lawless passion.

He possessed the sorcery of intrepid men ; he knew the signs that silence watch-dogs' barking, the magic words that force the invisible *djinns* to sweep the path clear of obstacles.

Naked as our father Adam, the sharp *flissa* between his teeth, he would glide into the tent where the fair one he had chosen for his favours awaited him in terror. Then close to the husband whose very breathing he could hear, he would enjoy in ample measure the sweets of stolen love.

After that he left the trembling woman, never to return. For this was his invariable habit ; never twice did he drink of the same cup. When the pitcher was flawed, he discarded it.

This he had sworn to do, sworn it by the fond memory of Meryem.

And the young envied him, and would say, when they saw him ride by on his beautiful mare *Oureka*, daughter of the black colt his father had given him :

"Look! look! the man who can command the *djinns*, and they obey!"

XXVIII.

BUT age came, a hated guest. Age came and knocked at his door one morning.

Mansour awoke with a start; he had been dreaming of his old father, and raising himself on his elbow, he found his limbs all stiff.

He was surprised, and asked himself what this might be. Then for the first time he noted that his beard was no longer black. One by one the hairs whitened, and his days grew dark with grief.

Till now he had never thought of counting the wrinkles under the *haïk* that hid his brow. The fancy took him to examine them, and standing before his mirror, a dumb inexorable witness, he pondered and marvelled what was the heavy plough that cut these furrows.

It was the plough of self-indulgence. No seed fills the furrows *it* makes, and no harvest ripens there!

One day a woman whom he had long been pursuing in vain, told him to his face, "You are an old man, leave me alone!"

So then, he was an old man,—he who had dreamed his youth would be eternal. Yes! he *must* be an old man, for a woman had dared to tell him so. Love had given him of its riches in exuberance; but here was bankruptcy at last. It was a stunning blow!

His brain was yet dizzy from its effects. What! was he, the "Happy Man," to be happy no longer? Was he, so long accustomed to bend Fortune to his caprices, was he to become in his turn the sport of caprice?

He would not, could not, believe it. He tried again in other quarters, but everywhere the reply was the same: "You are an old man!"

"It is a plot they have contrived to mock me," he thought. For he felt himself still young, in spite of grey hair and stiffened limbs. The body might have aged, but the heart had remained untouched, and was the heart of a young man of twenty.

However he found himself more and more isolated. All seemed to hate him; his old companions, his flatterers of former days, were now husbands and had long sedulously kept him at arm's length. A bachelor, childless and jealous of others' happiness, he saw himself the object of general distrust and dislike.

What was he to do? He had long regaled himself at the expense of his neighbours; now he must feast at his own cost and risk. Of a surety, notwithstanding the large hole twenty years of self-indulgence had made in his property, he was still rich enough to buy a wife, and a fair wife. But it was a matter for serious reflection.

He had had the laugh of so many husbands! would not he be made a laughing stock in his turn? Was he, intrepid and astute as he was, at last to find a master?

It is written, "He that hath betrayed, shall be betrayed; he that hath beaten, shall be beaten; he that hath robbed, shall *be* robbed; and he that hath polluted his neighbour's wife, the same shall fall asleep wrapped about with pollutions. Evil must needs be repaid by evil."

XXIX.

YET more than ever isolation and solitude weighed heavy upon him. He was weary of his roving life. Women wanted his favours no more, but he wanted and longed for the solace of a woman's presence.

"Man cannot live alone." He needs a gentle hand to soften his rugged exterior, the ray that shoots from a loving woman's eye to warm his hearth and brighten his life. The wise men of all times have said, "A man that is companionless must needs grope his way, and wander from the path; then he stumbles and rolls in the mire." For on the rough, dark road of life, it is ever the wife that holds the torch, the husband that takes the ead.

The thoughtless have said: "A wife's girdle is a girdle of vipers, and her hair is full of scorpions."

"A woman, 'tis the accursed thing."

Nay! she is only accursed because man has thrown on her the pollution of his lusts; the vipers of her girdle are but the creation of her master's passions.

"Man *must* not live alone." Nor yet must he sit silent but with envious eyes, a parasite on others' happiness. He must have a fireside of his own, wife and children of his own. Such is the law. An intruder at the fireside is as water to put out the fire.

Mansour realized all this, but too late. The man they called *happy* and *astute*, found himself wretched, and knew his cunning had been mere foolishness. His house was empty, and he felt his life to be as empty as his house.

His passing loves have left no more lasting trace behind than the flash of the drawn sword leaves in the air it cleaves.

In sooth he needs must take a wife. He would love her with a young man's love, the heart and vigour and energy of a young man. He would love her to the end, till his last hour sounded; then he would depart, saying: "There is no happiness I have not tasted!"

XXX.

BUT day after day he hesitated, full of doubt and apprehension.

What he dreaded was that he should not enhale the first perfume of the flower he would fain pluck to lend sweetness to his declining years.

To be deceived during marriage is shameful,—at least so the world thinks, attaching shame to an act

in which the sufferer has no part,—but to be deceived
before marriage! what a triply distilled shame!

To pay the price of a new piece of goods, and
find it damaged; to buy an orange whose juice
another has sucked; to cut a melon, and there is
nothing under the rind; to open a pomegranate
and lo! the pips are eaten; to pour one's happiness
in a goblet, and discover a crack in the glass!

This he would never do; he swore it by the
ashes of his father. But he forgot he had to reckon
with the eternal Justice of Heaven.

The prophet said: "The woman should be
humble and obedient. She should guard, when her
husband is abroad, the treasure that pertaineth to
him and to no other. Such a woman is virtuous,
she is the joy of her mate, the pride of her family,
and her acts are writ in the book of Good Works.
Honour her; she is equal in honour to the angels."

"Yes! but where is such a woman to be found?"

He had searched long, defying the law of the
Koran that punishes adultery. He had searched
from South to North, in the Sahara and in the
Tell, beneath the tent of the *Bedoui* and in the
stone house of the *Hadar*, and everywhere he had
found wives that were of easy virtue. With the
most prudish, success had been but a question of
address and time and money. Perhaps they were
the evil doors he knocked at, but at any rate he
heard each man say: "*My* wives at least are
faithful."

And for the maids, the same easy victory,—
heart and body ready to yield to the first who
presents himself. More, a man must present himself
in good time to *be* the first.

How hope to find a pure woman? Again and
again he had known men take for wives girls whose
honour he had bought, and had heard them boast
after the wedding-night: "My darling was as virgin-
pure as Lalla-Fathma."

The proud and happy husband spoke with con-
viction; and Mansour would say to himself with a
smile, "It is not in cities only there are matrons
possessed of cunning arts."

So he pondered, and forgotten incidents came
back to memory. There is ever a penalty to pay
for groping among the ashes of the past.

"Meryem! Meryem!"—The name came back to
him at once sad and sweet, a joy at once and a
sorrow.

He had hoped to obliterate its memory in the
wild orgies of his early manhood and the vigorous
passions of his maturity.

He had hoped to dig its grave for ever, to bury
its dead corpse and throw over its coffin, spadeful
after spadeful, the names of all the many mistresses
he had loved for an hour. He thought it well
buried and well forgotten, and lo! now his manhood
was on the wane, now he was already knocking
at the portals of old age, the memory of a sudden

arose from its grave, and throwing aside its shroud of oblivion, showed, not dead at all but alive and vengeful, the dread skeleton of his old sin,—" Meryem! Meryem!"

XXXI.

MERYEM! Meryem!—Fatal name that confronted him in all the fiercest storms of his life,—incest and adultery! treason and rape!

Meryem! Yes! but which Meryem? For there were two, both ruined by him, both forced by him from the path of virtue. His memory confused the two, when he thought of them, under the one sweet name Meryem, name of the Virgin undefiled!

He could not recall the face of the one, without the image of the other straightway springing to his memory.

Beginning and end, first act and last of his love-drama, first page and last of the book of his heart. All that came between seemed but as mire and foulness.

The last act! *Then* he was strong and vigorous; yes! he remembered it well. His beard was still black, and his leg muscular. He had already drunk deep of the cup of life; but women's eyes still smiled at him, and no one dreamed of telling him, " You are an old man!"

Was it so long ago? Nay! his memory of it all was fresh. Yesterday! it was a thing of yesterday!

Yet ten times since then the palm-trees of the *Beled-el-Djerid* had yielded the peaceful dweller of the plain his double harvest of dates. Ten years! a yawning chasm in life's course! a fleeting moment to look back on!

Yes! he remembered it all so well. The happy vision had vanished like a dream; but now it came back to his memory in clear and distinct outlines, and stood before him.

XXXII.

IT was evening. He was seated under one of the low walls that separate the gardens of *Msilah* from each other, engaged in deep and anxious thought, alone in the deserted path.

Suddenly the deep voice of the Muezzin sounded from aloft, slow and solemn. Mechanically he listened to the priest, who cried from the summit of the minaret to the four quarters of the horizon:

"There is no God but God. His are the East and the West; which way soever a man turneth himself, there shall he meet His face.

"God is one God; lift up your hearts and worship Him!"

Kneeling down and turning towards the East, his forehead bowed in the dust, he repeated the prescribed evening prayer. This done, he sat down once more, rested his back against the stones of the wall and watched between the stems of the palms

the purple cloudlets that floated in a golden haze
above the range of the blue Eastern hills.

A deep stillness reigned. The sounds of daily
life had one by one fallen silent in the *Ksour*; in
the gardens of the oasis he could hear the low calls
of the jackals that slipping through where the walls
had fallen, were beginning their nightly prowl in
search of food.

Of what was he dreaming? Perhaps of the fair
daughter of the Muezzin *El-Ketib*, whose voice had
called up her image to his mind. Men called her
the Pearl of the Ksour, and only the day before
he had seen her on the terrace of her father's house,
unveiled, with great dark eyes and breasts like a
houri. She was watering the pomegranates that
were in flower in the terrace-garden, and for a
quarter of an hour and more, he had watched her
graceful movements, hidden himself behind the trellis
of a window in his host's dwelling. Now stooping
over the great flower-pots, delicately pruning the
trees, now standing upright, with head bent over
the shoulder, she directed on the plants a thin stream
of water from an urn of red earthenware.

Presently, with careless step but with that delicious
swaying of the hips that marks a young girl when
she first begins to feel the time of love near, she
would go to the well to re-fill her *djouna* (water-pot).

He was a connoisseur to appreciate these charming
signs; he was not the man to be deceived in matters
of the sort!

Thus he found himself deeply enamoured. "I shall love that maiden," he said to himself, "more than all the rest; my heart shall be true to her." For indeed he always said so, whenever he coveted a new prey.

So from that very day, he began, as a cunning strategist should, to study the place he was to lay siege to.

The Muezzin, a one-eyed old man, miserly, pious and austere, guarded his daughter as the apple of his only remaining eye. She was his youngest, and in all probability he would not have another child. So having increased his substance by the rich *sadoukas* (marriage-gifts) given by the love-sick bridegrooms of his elder daughters, he was counting on the last, and fairest of all, to round off finally his capital. Accordingly he watched over her like a miser with a bag of gold.

But Mansour was not the man to be scared by obstacles and shirk an enterprise. In many a former adventure he had burst through more formidable barriers and braved greater dangers.

XXXIII.

HE was just calculating as he stood there in the bye-road, what might be the extreme price one of her waiting-maids would ask for her connivance in aiding him to gain access to her mistress, when he heard a light step approaching and caught sight

of a man, whom he seemed to recognize in spite
of the twilight.

It was the son of *El-Arbi-ben-Souafa*, once Caïd
of the Ouled-Amdou, whose flocks had been looted
by the Roumis. At dawn he had been a rich
and powerful chief, by sunset he was a poor man,
poor among the poorest. The young man was a
favourite with Mansour. His face was gentle and
pleasing in expression, and the calamity recently
fallen on his family added to the interest he in-
spired. He was barely twenty, and lacking any other
means of livelihood, he proposed to enlist with the
Mokalis of the Caïd of Msilah.

Mansour was on the point of accosting the young
man as he passed, when the latter suddenly stopped,
cast a look over the neighbouring gardens, but
without perceiving the Sheikh, then climbed the
wall.

" Ho! ho! " thought Mansour, " is his poverty so
extreme he must needs pilfer the pomegranates in
the Muezzin's garden? "

But he soon discovered his mistake, and under-
stood what fruit it was that Lagdar wanted to steal;
for after some confused and inaudible whispering,
he distinctly heard the words:

" Four hundred *douros!* He claims four hundred
douros, my white gazelle! Verily all the palms of
all the oases, all the flocks that graze the plains
of the Tell and the mares of the Ouled-Nayl to
boot, were not price enough for one of your glances;

were I the Lord of the Universe, I would spread it
for a carpet before your feet, to win one smile.
But for me, son of El-Arbi a ruined man,——where
does he suppose, your flinty-hearted father, where
does he suppose I can get four hundred *douros?*"

"Nay? I have never learned to count," said a
soft voice, that made Mansour tremble; "it is a very
large sum, is it,——four hundred *douros?*"

"It would buy four mares of the Haymour!"

"Allah help us!.. four mares of the Haymour!"

"And I that have not wherewithal to buy an
ass of Biskara."

"Lagdar, I am fain to be yours——for nothing!"

"Oh! joy of my eyes, moon of my soul, sun of
my heart, rose and perfume of my life, I thought,
I dared to think, you would say so...Well then!
we will fly. I will take you to the ksour of
El-Djema, to my mother's house. Let the Muezzin,
El-Ketib, come there and tear you from my arms,
if he can. Yes! we will fly. Had I to make the
journey on my knees over the sand with you in
my arms, I should find the way short and the
burden light."

"She is virgin still," said Mansour to himself.

"But we must act speedily," continued Lagdar;
to-morrow perhaps your father will close with some
rich wooer's offers. Every hour adds a stone to
the wall between us, and soon it will be impassable.
We must fly to-morrow. What says your heart?"

"My heart trembles, but it says Yes!"

" And your will?"

" I will what you will."

There was a moment's silence. But lips that lay on lips moved softly still, though no word was said.

" To-morrow then I will be here at the same hour, with a friend whose devotion I can trust, a man of the *Djebel-Sahari*. He will bring with him for you a grey mule whose pace is swift and sure, and please God, at sunrise we shall be at the *Ksour*."

" Please God it be so!"

" Now, let me taste the sweets of your lips once more."

They fell in each other's arms. It was long before they could tear themselves away; at last they separated, each with the murmured word " To-morrow".

Mansour, motionless in the shadow, stood aside to let the happy lover pass.

" Not a *boudjou* (farthing) in his pocket, and the creature dares to love!" he muttered. " Wait till you have earned some money to know the price of a woman. And I," he added bitterly,— "*I* am too late. The *Pearl of the Ksour* is another's. A curse on the young villain! I was too late for Meryem, who became my father's bride; and I am too late now!"

XXXIV.

NEXT day he was astir and in the great square of the *Ksour* when it was still very early. Already the sun was shining brilliantly, and he sat down in the shade of the penthouse in front of Ali-bou-Nahr's shop,—your humble servant. I was then making my first essays in the noble art of healing, a poor trade in the Souf, where the barbers and the farriers share the patients between them! So to employ my too abundant leisure, I used to write charms, and make copies of passages from the Koran in ornamental characters.

Mansour asked me for a light for his *chibouk;* and presently after watching for a while the blue coils of smoke as they rose slowly, and gradually disappeared in the clear morning air, said:

"Do you sell love-philtres, *Thebib* (Doctor)?"

"I sell everything,—love as well as hate, I write the magic words that turn bullets aside, and those that make men proof against the *flissa* of the injured husband. Faith is the great healer! But, what! Do *you*, Mansour, you that are known as the Happy Lover, do you need charms of the sort?"

He began to laugh, and said.

"Why, yes! sometimes."

"The best talisman is to be handsome and well-made."

"I know of a better still,—to be bold."

At the same moment a young man passed close by us, looking hurried and excited. Mansour accosted him:

"Lagdar-ben-El-Arbi, I thought you were already enlisted in the Mag'zen."

" No! not yet," replied Lagdar.

" Well, perhaps you did well to wait. Your father was my friend, and I wish well to you."

" Speak, sir! Your words are like yourself,— welcome."

" You know me, doubtless, by name, though I am not native of the *Ksour*, I am called Mansour-ben-Ahmed, but the *Thaleb* Ali-bou-Nahr yonder will tell you how the folk of the Tell and the men of the *Beled-el-Djerid* have added to my name the title of *Messaoud* (The Happy Man), because they say I succeed in whatever I undertake."

" Yes! I know," answered Lagdar.

" Good! Now listen. I am about to make another journey to the land of the Negroes. You are aware how full of danger and hardship such an undertaking is; therefore I need young men, who are hardy and resolute. I have thought of you. Will you go with me?"

"Your offer is a compliment, Mansour; and I thank you for it. When are you to start?"

" I am only waiting for my camels, that are due from Constantine with a freight of silk, *chechias* (bright-coloured kerchiefs), *burnouses* and *haïks*. If they arrive to-morrow, I shall rest the beasts one day, and then away."

" Alas! that makes it impossible," replied the young man, "I am very grateful for your offer, but I have an important matter that prevents my starting so soon."

" Important! and what can be more important than making your fortune? A fortune, I tell you, a fortune—with douros galore and golden sequins; the voyage will make your fortune! What more important business can there be, when one is twenty, —unless it be that curse of curses, love!"

Lagdar cast a look of indignation and pity on the profaner of so holy a name.

" You are filled with indignation and scorn for me, because *I* scorn love. You are young, and you presume on your ignorance. Yes! your ignorance; but beware lest knowledge come to you all too soon. I tell you, love—a *poor* man's love, is the bitterest of bitter things. Better expose the delicate form you love, without a shred of clothing, to the scorching rays of the sun and the bites of the mosquitoes than to the cold fang of poverty. Love will wane under the blight, and beauty fade; and her frozen hands will have no more caresses to bestow. When you would fain kiss her sunken lips, you will feel only the teeth in her fleshless gums, that tell of hunger.... Come, young sir! join my company, and you will soon find in the Soudan the four hundred *douros* a miserly father claims."

" By the nine and ninety names of Allah, who told you of this?" exclaimed the young man in amazement.

" Bah! I know all this, and many another thing beside, Lagdar-ben-El-Arbi. The folk of this land

6

call me the *Happy Man*, but the men of my own
tribe have long given me the honoured name of
Thalcb. I was not yet your age, when the old
men of the *Ouled-sidi-Abid* cried after me as I
left my home, '*Sidi-Thaleb*, we salute you.' Ah,
me! that is long ago, long ago!"

He let his chin fall on his breast, and involuntarily
his lips let fall the name of *Meryem*.

XXXV.

LAGDAR caught it, as he would a falling pearl.
He would have been glad to take it within his lips.

" Who told you her name?" he cried, furious that
another should have dared to utter it. " Speak, I
would know who it is mixes himself in my secrets."

Mansour raised his head.

"Did I speak her name? If I did, it was, I swear,
without intending to; the name escaped me, like a
bird that flies its cage. Would it might never come
back! But as you are angry and will have it, I
will tell you yet another thing. Come close; let
us speak low. You are to carry her off this very
evening at the hour of the *eucha.* * Come, come!
do not open your eyes so wide, like a Roumi
prisoner whose eyelids they have cut off. Better
listen to my advice: don't climb the Muezzin's
garden-wall again, or mayhap instead of his daughter's

* *Lalat-el-eucha*, the evening-prayer,—at eight o'clock.

gentle eyes you may find the point of a *flissa* to greet you. I have spoken."

"I have been betrayed. A curse on the villain that has spied on me and overheard my words. I shall know how to punish him!"

Mansour smiled to see the boy's beardless mouth big with threats, and said, "Better think how you may grow rich. Then you can buy the maid at the price her father asks, ... *if* you love her still, and you deem her worth four hundred *douros*."

"She is worth four thousand *douros*; and I shall love her forever."

"Four thousand is a large sum; and *forever,*—to love forever, ludicrous!"

"Ten thousand *douros* would be too small a price for her!"

"We will not go beyond four hundred," said Mansour with a sneer; "four hundred is a good sum. It makes two thousand francs, as the Roumis count money,—too heavy a price for a girl whose first favours you have enjoyed already."

"You lie," screamed Lagdar, trembling with rage, "you lie! Who told you the falsehood, who told you she had given herself to me? Who told you I had ever done more than kiss the velvet of her blushing cheek and the hem of her *gandourah?* The curse of the Prophet on your head, who dare to sully with your baseless calumnies the *Pearl of Msilah!*"

Mansour smiled afresh at the lover's furious indignation. It rejoiced his heart. " I was right, " he thought, " she is virgin yet. " Then aloud:

" Your anger pleases me, son of El-Arbi; I like to see a champion of women's honour. It shows a generous nature. Men of your age as a rule speak scornfully of women. They are of an easy virtue, the fair ones of the oases and the ksours; then because they have not respected their future bride themselves, young men say, 'Bah! respect! no woman deserves it!'"

" But we, older men who have seen more of life, and knocked in vain at many a door, we know the truth. Yes! by Allah, there *are* virtuous maids, and the Muezzin's daughter is one of them. She is worth the four hundred *douros!*.... Yet, four hundred *douros!* 'Tis a big sum, and a heavy one it takes long to save! Remember how her father has kept watch and ward over his daughter, in hope of the day when he should reap his reward. The labourer is worthy of his hire; and indeed a daughter's maidenhood is not kept safe without nights of wakefulness, and care and anxiety. The sower is entitled to expect a harvest, the sower of good no less than the sower of evil. The Muezzin has sown a wonder of the world; and would you rob him of the fruits?.... Son of El-Arbi, your father was an upright man; his motto was,—Every man should have his own. His words were straight-forward, and his actions corresponded to his words. Are you not his child? Why then, if you are, these

tortuous ways? Why try to cheat this old man of
his hopes? Why rob him at once of his daughter
and her *sadouka?* Ah! it is ever an easy thing
to seduce a maid and lead her into dark ways. The
ancient text says to the woman : 'Thou shalt leave
father and mother to follow after thy husband.'
But the command was futile, for it is written in the
Law of Nature from the beginning : 'There is no
maid but will leave father and mother to follow after
the first comer that has won her heart.' Your
victory is an easy one ; but this will not be so
easy,—to stifle your remorse hereafter. Remorse !
by our holy Prophet, I pray you may never know
what remorse is ! Remorse is a deadly poison that
withers the flowers of life, and destroys their beauty
and sweetness. Soon, the first transports over, the
sense of honour you inherit from your old father
El-Arbi will rise in revolt at the thought of the
hundred *douros*,—the *sadouka* you would rob an
old man of."

"I begin to think you are right."

"Will you stain your love, your first love, with
deceit? At the very moment of your first kiss, shall
your name be written down in the *Sid-djin**   along-
side those of knaves and swindlers? Shall fraud be
the *djinn* to preside over your marriage-night?
I swear by my head and by your own, that in the
very arms of your young bride, you will feel the

---

* Book in which are inscribed the evil actions of men. The Book
of the Righteous is the *Illiourn.*

weight of the stolen gold like a millstone round your neck."

"Your words are of good counsel; speak on, I will do as you bid me."

"I have merely to repeat my former offer. I said I would take you with me to the land of the Negroes, and I will. If you know your own good, you will accompany me, and we will return with the *sadouka* to buy your bride."

"And how long will this journey last?"

"Six months at longest, and you will be a rich man."

"Six months! By then the Muezzin will have given her to another. She is almost a woman; she will soon be fourteen!"

"Be not afraid. It is not every day a suitor can be found in the *Beled-el-Djerid* able to give four hundred *douros* for .... a girl's bright eyes."

"Oh! he will find wooers. He will find wooers ready to pay more than that."

"Well then! I will do more for you than give you a piece of empty advice. I am anxious to secure you, and I am willing to advance you a hundred *douros* on the future gains of our enterprise. This sum you can pay by way of instalment to the Muezzin."

"Can I believe my ears? You would do me such a kindness, most righteous and most generous of true Believers!"

"Come at the hour of the *eucha*; I will count

you out your hundred *douro*s, and you can go and
knock at the old man's door without another
instant's delay. Never fear but they will open.
The door always flies open to the visitor who car-
ries a bag of money. Her father will be only too
glad to take the gold, and will find himself pledged
to the bargain."

"The *eucha*, did you say? But I had fixed that
as the trysting hour! Cannot you choose another?"

"No! that is the only time I can find. I have
business all day long. Is it agreed?"

"But I tell you, Meryem will be there, and I
have neither time nor opportunity to warn her of
the change of plan."

"Well then! let her wait. Delay will only make
her more fond, especially when she learns why
she has had to wait."

"My father!" cried the young man, eagerly kissing
the hem of Mansour's *burnouse*, "may Allah's bless-
ing and the Prophet's meet on your kind head;
may you ever till the last moment of your life
deserve your surname of *the Happy Man!*"

"Be punctual! So soon as the last syllables of
the Muezzin's call have rung out in the evening
air, knock at my door. Punctuality is twin-sister
of success."

"Please God, I shall be there."

XXXVI.

•

IT was twilight. The Muezzin's voice had ceased; and in the great square, at the corners of streets, by the fountain, everywhere, standing, kneeling or prostrated full-length on the ground, men turned their faces to the East. "For every man hath one region of the sky to the which he turneth;" but the East is the holy temple, the fountain-head of the World. Under the rays of the Eastern sun have germinated the seeds of things, and the nations of the Earth developed.

Arms crossed over the breast or raised before the face, the Faithful directed their thoughts to the Master of twilight and of daybreak. It was the silent, solemn hour allotted to prayer and adoration.

The vast profile of the minaret towered a white mass against the darkening sky. The palms showed their shaggy heads beyond the terraces, while between their black stems still flared the glories of the sunset. Storks poised on one leg, motionless as eternity itself, stood asleep on the edges of the roofs, high above the silent, praying people; and women's shadowy forms glided without a sound along the whitened walls.

At that moment there was a knock at the door of the house where Mansour dwelt.

Some minutes elapsed; then the usual questions and answers:

" Who is there?"

" A man."

" Who are you?"

" Lagdar-ben-El-Arbi."

" What do you want?"

" I want Mansour-ben-Ahmed."

" You wish to speak with him?"

" Yes! if God will."

" Tell me your name again."

" Lagdar-ben-El-Arbi."

" Wait."

A boy introduced the visitor into the little paved vestibule, with stone benches, that intervenes between the street and the inner courtyard, and which no foreigner ever goes beyond.

" Sit down," said the lad to Lagdar, " I will call Mansour."

He shut the door carefully; then in a moment two or three women called one after the other, in melancholy tones:

" Mansour! Sidi-Mansour! Master! Mansour-ben-Ahmed! *Ia Radjel!* Master! Sidi-Mansour-ben-Ahmed!"

Sidi-Mansour-ben-Ahmed not answering, the door opened again, and the boy begged the visitor to wait an instant longer.

So Lagdar waited, devoured by impatience, for the *instant* was of great length. He could not help saying to himself he would have had time twice over to keep his appointment with Meryem;

however he was still full of reliance on Mansour, and listened eagerly to the faintest sounds within or without the house. At every footstep that came near, he would get up and say, "Here he is at last," and it was only after spending an hour thus, a weary unprofitable hour, that vague suspicions first crossed his mind.

Then the demon with the sharp claws, called Anxiety, set on him and tortured him unmercifully.

He knocked again, and shouted:

"Ho! you women there, is Mansour-ben-Ahmed within?"

The voices began again with their melancholy cadence:

"Mansour! Sidi-Mansour! *Ia Radjel!* Master! Mansour-ben-Ahmed! Sidi-Mansour-ben-Ahmed! Master!"

Followed by confused noises. Steps could be heard going up and down the stone stairway; then an old woman called from a high balcony:

"What is your name?"

"Lagdar-ben-El-Arbi."

"What do you want?"

"I want to speak with Mansour-ben-Ahmed, if God so will."

"He is not here; he has gone out on affairs of business, but he said he would come back."

Lagdar was furious, and refusing to wait another minute rushed from the house. Perhaps he might even yet find Meryem at the tryst? But he ran against a tall negro, who seized him by the shoulder and stopped him.

XXXVII.

"ARE you Lagdar-ben-El-Arbi?"

"I am."

"God be praised! you are the man I seek."

"Do you bring me a message from Mansour?"

"Ah! mother of the Prophet! ah! blessed paps that he sucked! Mansour-ben-Ahmed, did you say? —Mansour the Happy, Mansour father of the musket, Mansour master of the sword, Mansour the *Thaleb*. Yes! Mansour is my master, the poor black man's master, Mansour has not his match. You must travel far—to Constantine, perhaps to holy Algiers, who knows? to find the like of Bou-Zeb. For they call him *Bou-Zeb* too. Ah! ah! Did you know that?"

"Yes! Yes! but be quick. What did he tell you to say?"

"I am as silly as a sheep. I ask you if you know Mansour! Why! who does not know Mansour in all the Tell and the Beled-el-Djerid?"

"Explain, explain. What message did he charge you to give me?"

"He told me, 'Salem',—my name is Salem,— 'you are to go to Lagdar-ben-Arbi, who is waiting at my house.' But *are* you Lagdar-ben-Arbi?

Look you, it is so easy to cheat me! I am a stranger in the *Ksour*, like my master; and we poor ignorant negroes, we believe everything we are told."

"Go into the street, ask the first passer-by, and he will tell you my name."

"Well, well! I see you are the man. Now, what am I to give you?"

"*You*! I don't know. I am waiting for your master, who is to give me a hundred *douros*."

"A hundred *douros!* mother of the Prophet! a hundred *douros!* The poor black man will never have such a sum as that. If I owned a hundred *douros*, I would buy all the girls in the Soudan."

"Be quick! I say. Man! be quick."

"Oh, yes! I was sure you were the man. Now, look here; if I were bringing you a hundred lashes, you wouldn't be so impatient. Oh, yes! you are the man. Praise the Prophet's name! I was praying all the way as I came along that he would make me find you without a long search; for my master, look you! said just what you do, 'Be quick!'"

"You don't follow his orders any more than you do mine."

"What! don't you see how fast I've come? Why! I run water like a fountain in a thirsty land. Yes! I am a fountain of running waters. But lo! I tasted myself, and I was salt. By the mother of Aïssa (Jesus), who was a virgin like mine the day that she conceived me, the camels would not look at me! Ha! ha!"

" To business, man, to business! for God's sake."

" The business is thuswise: My master, he said to me, 'You see this bag, Salem?—Yes! master. —There are a hundred *douros* in it.--Yes! master. —You are to carry them .... —Yes! master—To the man called Lagdar-ben-El-Arbi.—Yes! master.' Then away I went, but he called me back, and I came back, and he said to me, said he, 'You will add these words: You are to do as we agreed.'"

" And that is all?"

" That is all. So here I am. I have told you the words; and here are the hundred *douros*."

And he drew from under his *burnouse* a leather bag. He grinned and shook it, and it gave out a merry rattle of money.

" Plenty to buy all the maids in the Soudan! Ha! ha! ha!" Then he began to dance and sing, waving the bag over his head:

> " A hundred dollars,—a hundred maids!
> Seven times seven
> The joys of heaven!
> A hundred dollars,—a hundred maids!"

" Drunken beast!" cried Lagdar, "then it was you who kept me waiting so long. You stopped in some pot-house on the way; you stink of anisette." *

" God of Heaven, that I should hear such things! *I*, who never in all my life drunk anything but

* A liquor extracted from onions, commonly known by the name of *anisette juive*.

spring-water, I ran my best, I tell you; it is the sweat you smell."

Lagdar put his hand on the bag.

"No! no! no!" said the negro quickly, "we must count the money first."

"Needless. Stink as you may of strong drink, like a Christian, yet I will trust you. If you have spent a *douro* by the way, I make you a present of it."

"By the four breasts of my two wives! Ask me to give you my head, but don't ask me to give you the bag, before we have counted the *douros!* You might lose one or two, and then you would say: The villain has robbed me. God be my witness, I would not pick up a date that had dropped from the tree! My skin is black, but I have a white conscience. I will count the coins before your eyes."

XXXVIII.

AH! my son, it was a long and arduous under-taking! First of all a light had to be fetched; then when after much talking and many difficulties one was obtained at last, he emptied out the bag on the stone bench so roughly that a considerable number of the coins rolled away in every direction.

Lagdar boiling with impatience the while, the negro groped after them on the floor, loudly cursing his own clumsiness; finally, when he thought he had recovered them all, he proceeded to arrange them in little piles of three.

"That's not the way to count money," cried Lagdar, "that's not the way" ....

"Hands off, let me do it my own way. There, you've made me lose count!"

So saying, he started afresh, this time with piles of six.

"Count by fours," said Lagdar.

"Oh! let me do it my way! I have a way of counting of my own; I'm not a mathematician! There now, you've made me lose count again!"

He got more and more confused. First it was 98 *douros*, then 97. He finished up by making it only 80.

Finally Lagdar cried, trembling with rage:

"Put it all back in the bag, fellow; I will take what there is, and not complain."

"But my master would drive me from his service. I *have* drunk a drop, look you, on the road. Needs must allow it, as you find I smell of anisette; but by my mother's womb, that will never, never bear another like me, I swear, and by your mother's head, I have not touched one of your crowns. Listen, listen! I am going to tell you how it was. I tasted strong drink for the first time in my life, yes! the first time in all my life,—just one little drop of anisette."

"No need, fellow! your tales are nothing to me. Come now, hand over the *douros!*"

" Never! unless *you* verify the total while I look
on, for I see well enough I shall never get it right.
Yes! *you* count the money, my son. I want you
to leave this house, your mind free of all suspicion.
Count it yourself, count it yourself ! "

Lagdar set to work, and found there were only 99.

" I will not complain, " he said as he threw the
coins into the bag again. " I will take them as a
hundred. Farewell. "

" No! no! Sidi, stop. No true Believer has ever
suspected me of theft. My master gave me a
hundred *douros,* and a hundred *douros* I must hand
over to you.... Stop! stop! ah! here it is. The
coin must have been bewitched; here it is under
my *sebate.* Without a doubt it was an evil *djin*
hid it there. By the paps of my mother I sucked
as a babe, by the soft bosoms of my wives, it is
a devil's *douro.* If I were you, I should not put
it back with the others ; I should throw it to some
beggar. "

Lagdar, overjoyed to be done with it all at last,
tossed him the coin, and fled.

XXXIX.

FROM the time he entered Mansour's lodging to
the moment when the negro, laughing in his sleeve,
finally bolted the door behind him, all but two
hours had slipped by. The *Ksour* lay asleep. In
the great Square big brown camels crouched by the

side of their loads, motionless with outstretched
necks, while the drivers, lying wrapped in their
burnouses at full length on the dry ground, forgot
in sleep the fatigues of the past day and those they
had yet to face. He took it to be the caravan
Mansour had spoken of, and the sight made him
run all the faster towards the gardens, full as he was
of a lover's sanguine hopes. He thought he would
even now find Meryem there in waiting for him.
It grieved him to imagine the girl's anxiety, and he
could not help saying to himself that the hundred
douros he held pressed to his breast, earnest of a
future happiness, were a poor equivalent to set
against her present suspense and the tears her bright
eyes must be shedding.

Who would exchange the delights of immediate
possession, he thought, for the promise of others
still in the future and uncertain? If he had never
met Mansour, at this very moment he would have
his mistress clasped to his heart instead of his bag
of *douros*. She would be lying warmly enfolded
in his protecting arms, happy and trusting, each
wrapped up in the other, no witnesses by but the
stars and the far-stretching plains. He would close
her eyes with the kisses of his mouth, while the
faithful mule bore them swift and sure over the
desert-sands.

Present happiness! Yes! let us keep it, whilst
it is ours,—keep it close guarded in our heart, close
as the love of the first well-beloved; and never

expose it to the ever-changing caprice of that hungry, faithless thief men call To-morrow!

Fools, that hope to lay up in the garners of the future a store of happy hours! The storehouses of the future are built in the clouds. They vanish at the first puff of wind; the first storm disperses them. Enjoy the passing moment wisely and well; it alone is yours to enjoy. To-morrow is in the hands of God, who has numbered the hours of your life.

Lagdar was a fool, and ran to catch the very happiness he had under his hand all the while. He put off drawing his bill to another day, as if a man should make Fate his broker, and peddle with his life's happiness. He ran through the deserted streets, where none was abroad, save perhaps his evil genius following on his heels with a mocking laugh.

A few starving dogs were prowling about, and slunk away to let this untimely disturber of the peace pass by; others were sawing with their hungry teeth at the bones the half-famished camel-men had gnawed already, and hearing his hurried steps and dreading to lose their meagre feast, fled growling along under the grey walls.

He left behind him the lofty minaret of the mosque, that towered into the dark sky like a tall *genie*, and seemed to be keeping watch and ward over the little town sleeping below so peacefully amid the vast solitude of the desert.

XL.

PANTING with haste, he reached the maze of narrow
roads intersecting the oasis. Arrived there he
slackened his speed, and gliding behind the wall
of the Muezzin's garden, listened. The same deep
silence as in the lonely streets reigned amid the
greenery of the enclosures.

"Meryem! Meryem!"—but there was no answer.

He was more annoyed than really anxious. She
could not of course have waited for him till so late.
The evening star already blazed high in the heavens,
and the hour of the tryst was long past. He
climbed the wall, and walked up and down in the
garden.

"Meryem! Meryem!" he called again in a low
voice, but he was alone in the garden.

Some jackals barked in the distance; and troubled
and thoughtful he turned homewards, What was
it made him sad? He possessed a hundred *douros*,
—a deposit imposing enough to certainly insure the
Muezzin's consent; he would come back from the
Soudan a rich man to win the pearl of Msilah.
What made him sad, when the future shone so
bright?

He was sad, because the future was still distant,
—eight months distant, and eight months are two
hundred and fifty to-morrows. How many hours
and cares and surprises and uncertainties in eight

months! He was young, strong and bold. He feared no fatigue, he feared neither thirst nor the *Simoom*, neither foe nor any other peril. But like all lovers he was fain to enjoy at once; he had happiness in his grasp, and had let it go,—perhaps for ever!

A traveller knows the hour of departure; but who can foretell with certainty the hour of his return?

XLI.

HE slept but little, and dawn found him astir. He regretted not having followed Mansour's advice to carry the deposit at once to the old man; and dreamed some more fortunate wooer anticipated him. So the storks were only just awake, and the sun's earliest rays slanting down on the tiled roofs and touching the white terraces of the Ksour, when Lagdar started for the Muezzin's abode, his bag of gold under his *burnouse*.

But as he drew near, he heard the loud voices and clamour of a crowd.

Notwithstanding the early hour the street was full of people, conversing in excited groups of some event, the very mention of which made the young man shudder. He was still trying to understand, yet afraid to enquire, when the door burst open, and the Muezzin, with crimson face and swollen cheeks, his bald head bare and his eyes blood-shot, appeared on the threshold. His bony fingers tore at his .white beard as he cried:

"Robbed! I am robbed! Meryem! my sweet Meryem, pearl of the Oasis! Five hundred *douros*. I had refused five hundred *douros* for her, my sons! And now I lose both at once, my money and my child. Justice, honest friends, justice! Will you stand by and see a father robbed? I know the culprit,—that cursed jackal, that thief and vagabond I refused her to, Lagdar. Lagdar, that dog Lagdar, the Caïd El-Arbi's son. Khaoui-ben-Khaoui! .... Bankrupt and bankrupt's son. I tell you he has secreted her in a vile house kept by a hideous old procuress. To the rescue, my sons! Men of Msilah, to the rescue!"

And through the open door the women's piercing cries could be heard, screaming all at once like a flock of crows gone mad:

"To the rescue! to the rescue!"

And a tall negro brandishing a great stick cried louder than all the rest. "To the rescue!"

XLII.

IT was an old, old memory, but Mansour delighted in recalling it. He saw the whole scene again, as if it had happened yesterday, for his faithful negro had told him all that took place. Ha! ha! he laughed still when he thought of the trick he had played Lagdar. Then he sighed, for he saw once

more the gentle form of Meryem.   Almost featureless
at first, the shape gradually came back to him
clearer and clearer.   Meryem! the last of his loves!
The *first* he could not recall so distinctly, if he tried.

A hundred *douros!* He had paid a hundred *douros*
for the glorious maid!   What a sum; why! he
would gladly give a thousand now.   Lagdar had
spoken truth; she was a maid indeed, as pure as
the other Meryem (Mary) before she bore the Prophet
Aïssa, whose name the Roumis absurdly corrupt·
into Jesus, and worship him as the son of God!

God is one and unique.   How should he have
a son?

The Christians are fools and idolaters, for they
bow down before a piece of wood.   They worship
it and kiss it, and say, " It is God."

Mansour, without being a Christian, had become
an idolater; he idolized his own passions under the
name of Meryem.

She had made him forget the first Meryem, and
had remained long the object of his adoration.

Away! away, over the boundless desert!

God of Heaven! what a night of wild intoxica-
tion, there in the vast solitude of the desert, when
far enough away to defy pursuit, he halted at the
fountain of *El-Abiod* and lifted her from his mule,
half dead with fatigue and terror.

There, six hours' ride from the Oasis, at the foot
of the three palms that are still to be seen standing
sentry over the precious water of the well, under

the stars fading before the first gleams of morning-
light, he had revelled in all the intoxicating delights
of sin.   He lay bosom to bosom with her on the
tufts of the *diss*, twining his arms about her body,
biting her dark tresses.   The girl wept and cried
for mercy, fighting bravely for Lagdar and defend-
ing her virtue with all the strength she possessed;
but in vain.   Tears and screams were of no avail;
they roused not an echo, dying away unheeded and
unheard over the desert sands.

She called, " Lagdar! Lagdar!" but it was Mansour
that answered.   At length worn out by the useless
struggle, she yielded to the victor.   When the first
ray of the sun slanted over the distant hills that
quivered on the Eastern horizon, the Muezzin's child
had long ceased to resist.   Mounted on the saddle
before the master who had vanquished her and now
held her pressed to his breast, she silently wept for
the love she had left behind,—her poor timid lost
love.   She was terrified, yet submissive before the
resistless fate that tore her from her former lover's
arms for ever.

XLIII.

HE carried her far away, hiding her for three
months in the cities of the Tell, at Batna, afterwards
at Setif, finally at Constantine.   Maybe she had
ended by loving her unscrupulous overbearing lover,
and had forgotten the gentle Lagdar?   At any rate

she never spoke of him. She grew reconciled to
her life, and one evening announced that she was
about to be a mother. At this news, news that
makes a husband's heart leap with joy, and causes
him to redouble his fond attentions to the woman
he loves, Mansour frowned.

And next morning, at the City Gate, he enquired
as to caravans that might be leaving for the Souf.

Some days later he put Meryem in a palanquin
and rode by her side on horseback as far as the
outskirt of the Beled-El-Djerid.

"Go back to your father," he said, placing in the
litter a heavy leather bag, "look! the price of your
sadouka." Then kissing her a last time on the
mouth, he entrusted her to the care of the camel-
men and bade her farewell.

XLIV.

IT is written in the Book: "Slay not your children
through fear of poverty. To do after this wise is
murder, and a mortal sin."

But the father who abandons to the chances of
life the child he has begotten on a woman commits
a sin equally mortal, and more cruel and abomin-
able. Nor had Mansour the excuse of poverty; but,
like many another, he sought love, but shunned its
responsibilities.

"Children," he would say, "are ungrateful and
greedy. They have no memory for past kindnesses;

and are an inexhaustible source of tears and vexations for their parents."

Then he shook his head, thought no more of the matter, and started in search of fresh adventures.

Well! one night as he was riding across the plain of Djenarah to pay a visit to his brother the Caïd, a man darted from a clump of brushwood, leapt to his side, and stabbing him full in the chest cried:

"My name is Lagdar-ben-El-Arbi."

At early dawn some camel-drivers found him lying in a pool of blood. Death is a poll-tax levied on us all, but often we forestall the debt. However for once the Spectre that gathers in the taxes of God, glanced at the prostrate man and passed by on the other side.

Mansour returned to consciousness in his brother's house. A *Tebib* was bending over him, rehearsing the healing words of a charm, while a young negro woman he had brought from the Soudan seconded the holy man's efforts by pouring over the wound a decoction of flowers she had herself gathered.

He was often delirious, and asked for Meryem.

But no one knew the daughter of the Souf.

Then he cried: "Meryem! Meryem!"

"Hush! hush!" said the negress, "there are as fair maids in the Tell."

But he went on without hearing what she said:

"Meryem! Meryem! why must you be a mother? Children! I wanted no children!"

"Hush!" said the negress, "your words make you feverish."

She passed her hand softly over his forehead and eyes, till he fell asleep, still murmuring, "Meryem!"

Since his separation from her, the name of the young mother he had deserted had been but seldom on his lips, but the blow of Lagdar's dagger seemed to have awakened a more lively regret.

The thought that his rival now possessed the girl, having taken her of his own free will spite of desertion and disgrace, made his heart sore within him, and he lay groaning heavily on his bed.

"My lord!" the negress would say, "are you not *Sidi-Messaoud?*"

"The Happy Man! Happy! Oh! yes, you are right, my dusky beauty. Your words are soft and sweet as evening twilight; you are beautiful as a night of stars. When I am well, I will rest me on your ebon bosom, and forget my lost love."

"You are my lord and master,—all powerful."

He was long unable to rise from his bed; and when fever kept him awake and restless, he would repeat over and over again the loved name of the Muezzin's daughter.

This was his last intrigue. Death had come so close, it made him thoughtful and afraid. He grew more prudent, if not less vicious, and like a self-centred selfish bachelor, henceforth bought his pleasures,—the easy pleasures of an hour.

Then he made the pilgrimage to Mecca, and after grovelling on the tomb of the Prophet, came back a holy man.

But the lessons of maturity are powerless to affect life! They vanish at the first breath of passionate desire, like nests shattered by the hurricane.

XLV.

Now that he thought of all this, now that his memory went back to this drama of love long since forgotten, he beheld once more the lovely form of the maiden he had carried off one summer night in spite of father and of lover, and he was filled with longing.

It was such a woman as this he needed,—a virgin, undefiled in body, immaculate in mind, young, fair, gentle, loving and docile. But to find her? What land contained a treasure such as this? What roof of skins or of slates sheltered such a wonder of the world? What mat or what carpet was trodden by her naked feet?

Long he sought. He traversed the Tell and the Beled-El-Djerid. He visited the *douars*. He made enquiries in the towns. He conferred with the matrons. He was no longer young, but he was rich, and he soon perceived they were all eager to exploit him. They would have foisted on him girls that had been deflowered, nay! women debased by the life of the streets; but the same good luck, that from his youth up had ever sat by his side and ridden with him on every enterprise, remained his faithful comrade and saved him again and again from ridiculous mistakes.

The more he delayed, the more numerous grew his grey hairs, the more doubtful and difficult became the attainment of his object. But he only grew more obstinate, and would repeat over and over again, " I will find her yet."

As we get old, we get foolish.

At the last he had a wise thought: "The most astute are often deceived. In matters of the sort, 'tis chance is master. Why search and select? Truth is often found false, and falsehood true. Life is a mill-wheel, ever turning, turning; and a woman one of those light sheets of metal that men of the North set up on the roof of their houses to tell them the quarter of the wind. With women, to-morrow is the direct contradiction of to-day. Sweet girls often make bitter-tempered wives, the shy and shrinking grow brazen-faced, the modest fling aside their veil, and the bazars where harlots congregate are thronged with the virgins of yesterday. To count on a woman is to count on the passing cloud,—to say to the chameleon, 'Change colour no more.' A fool the man who declares, 'My wife will be so and so to-morrow.' We must needs choose at random; at any rate we will endeavour to secure a virgin."

Now there was only one way to be sure. Useless

to rely on the matrons he consulted. He deter-
mined to take his bride from the cradle; and this
he did.

A beautiful girl of the great tribe of the *Ouled-
Nayl*, famous for its beauties, died in giving birth to a
female child. The father had just fallen, face to the
foe, in the bloody actions of the Babors, and grief
rather than the dangers of childbirth had killed the
young mother.

Mansour announced that he would adopt the
child; and the family, who to their annoyance had
seen themselves saddled with an orphan's maintenance,
said at once:

"Generous man, she is yours."

Softly wrapped in *haïks* he bore her away on
his horse.

"This is my bride," he cried, as he looked at
her, his eyes full of tenderness, "this is my little
bride. In fourteen years from this day I will take
the child to my bed."

And with hand extended towards the East, he
uttered this solemn oath:

"By the Lord of the Dawn! by the Koran, all
glorious! by the Holy Caaba-stone! I swear; on
the sacred head of the Prophet! on the memory of
the two women I have loved, Meryem! Meryem!
I swear; I swear I will wed her a virgin still.
May I be for ever accursed if I come near her
before the appointed time! May I be for ever
accursed if any ravisher rob me of my bride! Ah!

he will have to be a cunning robber. I swear,
if he succeeds, I will fall at his feet, I will kiss the
hem of his garment and I will salute him my Lord
and Master!"

SECOND PART

THE VIRGIN BRIDE

"How beautiful are thy feet with shoes, O prince's daughter! The joints of thy thighs are like jewels, the work of the hands of a cunning workman; Thy navel is like a round goblet, which wanteth not liquor; thy belly is like an heap of wheat set about with lilies: Thy two breasts are like two young roes that are twins. Thy neck is a tower of ivory; thine eyes like the fishpools in Heshbon, by the gate of Bathrabbim ; thy nose is as the tower of Lebanon, which looketh toward Damascus. Thine head upon thee is like Carmel, and the hair of thine head like purple: How fair and how pleasant art thou, O love, for delights!"

SOLOMON'S SONG.

THE VIRGIN BRIDE

I.

HE dismissed his servants, both men and maids, keeping only the negress who had tended his wound and watched over his nights of delirium. She was twenty, and loved him with the devotion of a dog for its master; he had but to cast his eye on her, and she was ready to kiss his feet. She performed every duty of service,—made *couscous* and cakes, sweetmeats and perfumes, washed the linen and saddled the horse. A submissive slave to his slightest caprice, she would introduce without a murmur the mistress that was to share his couch for the night; then when he was sated with white women and longed after the bitter-sweet savour of the negress, at a sign she would be in his bed, proud to be there and ready to satisfy every wish he expressed.

Under her master's eye, she suckled the child and was its first nurse. While the rosy cheeks of the babe nestled to the copper-coloured bosom of the slave and the tiny hands pressed the black breasts, Mansour would sit by, smoking his long pipe with its bowl of red earthenware. As vigilant as *Mabrouka* herself, he watched over the sleeping infant, alert and restless, astir at the slightest cry, careful as a mother, and were such a thing possible, supplying a mother's place.

This made his happiness, a happiness he guarded like a miser's treasure, a happiness that grew and blossomed gloriously beneath his eyes, a budding flower of future joy.

But so soon as the child could stand and run to him with outstretched arms and little cries of delight, he sent the weeping nurse away to his brother's house, for he said,

" A woman will ever corrupt a woman."

II.

IT was then he built the country house, or *haouch* as we call it, that you see not far from the marshes of *Ain-Chabrou*, a half day's journey from *Djena-rah*, the *Pearl of the Souf*, where his brother, younger son of his mother Kradidja, was Caïd.

His desire was to live alone, aloof from the traffic of the roads, " far from Sultans ",—the dream of every Arab; far too from enviers and scorners, the inquisitive and jealous,—the aspiration of every wise man. Especially his wish was to guard the girl from the impure communications of the *douar* and the yet more impure examples of the cities.

For even with a mother and faithful attendants to watch over it, a child learns many things that were better hidden from it for its own good. A glance, a word, a gesture, are enough to tarnish the purity of a soul. The impression once received, remains branded as with a red-hot iron .on the mind, and is never effaced. The remembrance is a seed of evil in the mind. that grows as the mind grows.

So, like a wise man who has learned prudence from experience, he arranged a regular plan of action to follow: "This fair flower," he determined, "shall never suffer blight; no grub shall ever foul its half-opened bud. Rose of my old age, it shall enfold my last hours in light and fragrance. Till the happy night when I shall bear her to my bed, she shall be virgin as the *houris* of Paradise."

III.

HENCEFORTH all his aspirations, ambitions, desires, unsatisfied till now, every emotion and every anxiety, all centred in the child. The sweet little dark face had expelled from his heart the former evil, gloomy thoughts. It seemed to diffuse around a cheerful radiance that chased away the black shadows of regret for the past.

There was nothing in his surroundings to divert

his attention. His love wrapped her about in a warm embrace; and he thought he would be able to interpose between her and the external world so soft an atmosphere of perfumes and caresses and happiness that, even as she grew older, she would have no wish to look beyond it.

At times, as she was playing on the threshold of the *haouch*, he would call her, and the child would run to him all smiles. Then he would take her on his knee, pass his hand over her brow, measure the length of her tresses, see his image reflected in her great dark eyes, smile back at her smiling lips, red as two open pomegranates, examine the white pearls of her mouth. He loved to hold her little bare feet, ensconced in his hand, and to lull her to sleep by singing some old ditty of the Tell; and the child feeling love all about her, smiled at life, and fell gently asleep lapped in the warm shelter of so much love and care. Gaiety radiated from her presence, like light from the sun, brightening all around her. From the first moment she woke in the morning, the floodgates of happiness were opened; the little house rang with her merry laugh, and sunned itself in her smiles. The dog gambolled round her, the hens cackled noisily at her feet, the cock clapped his brilliant wings and crew lustily, the sparrows chirped, the blackbird from the nearest tree piped *Salamelek! Salamelek!* when it saw her; while even the she-goat, her second nurse, came up bounding and skipping, as

soon as she called out with her fresh voice *Maaza !
Maaza !*

The world basked in the light of her great eyes,
and Mansour felt his heart swell within him and
realized that for the first time he actually deserved
his name of *the Happy Man*.

IV.

BEHIND and on either side of the *haouch* there
was a little garden that grew as the child grew,
fenced in with a hedge of Barbary figs. The brook
that trickled from the foot of the mountain watered
it on its way, before it finally lost itself among the
reeds of the marsh. An hour or two's digging, a
few plants and a handful of seeds, changed a mere
mass of briars into the garden of Eden. Water-
melons and pomegranates, oranges and vines, mul-
berries and jujube-trees, grew luxuriantly and ca-
priciously as chance had willed when they were
planted, and kindly nature threw her magic cloak
of beauty over all.

From the warm virgin soil flowers sprung abundant,
strong and fragrant, in a picturesque confusion and
a sort of orderly disorder.

Flowers, vegetables and fruit,—they asked nothing
more. But the Caïd sent them from time to time
couscous as white as rice and dates of Biskara.
When Mansour wanted a sheep, he sent to inform
his brother. Then one was chosen from the great

flock that fed in the valley to northward of Djenarah.

Now and again, to amuse the child or to make some purchase, he used to visit the town. On such occasions he entrusted the care of the *haouch* to one of the camel-men whose *mahara* cropped the tufted *chichh*-grass of the plain; gave him two *sordis*, a *settla* full of *couscous*, or perhaps the head of a sheep, as provisions, and started in perfect security.

Besides, he had obtained three watch-dogs to guard the house, dogs of the famous man-eating breed, a cross between the hounds of the oasis and she-wolves. They spring at the horse's belly, without any fear of the rider, bite the stick he tries to beat them off with, and soon tear him in pieces. The unhappy marauder is devoured, the savage creatures growling and fighting over his carcase.

With such sentinels, thieves kept their distance as well by night as by day. Moreover they were aware neither *douros* nor precious stuffs nor jewels were to be found there; for Mansour's *douros* lay safely in the *fondouks* of his brother the Caïd, and his chief wealth consisted in the fat flocks that fed on the farther side of the *Djebel*. The only treasure in the *haouch* was the little Afsia; and in our markets this sort of jewel finds no sale.

So he would carry the child to the town, seated in front of him on his good mare or on the *berda* (pack-saddle) of his mule. Passers-by would point to the pair with a laugh and say to one another:

"Look! there is Sidi-Messaoud and his destined bride!"

But he answered angrily:

"Why, yes! it *is* my bride, and my bride will be a virgin bride on the marriage morning. Sons of Fathma, can you affirm as much of your own? Can you, children of the devil, swear the same of your daughters and your sisters?"

Then shrugging their shoulders and laughing louder:

"*Adda Maboul!*" they would cry, "The man is mad."

But others added:

"Nay! the finger of God has rested on his brow. My sons, mock him not. He shall ever deserve, till the day he dies, his surname of El-Messaoud.

V.

MEANWHILE his destined bride grew straight and tall, like a young palm-tree, though slender and delicate at first, yet giving ample evidence what a dainty morsel she would be anon.

Once again the *Happy man* showed himself well-named; for it might easily have happened that the child grew up uncomely. But in truth she already displayed a very perfect beauty,—dainty-sweet and gracious as the Sultanas our poets sing of, beautiful as the *houris* your painters of the West depict.

A dream of loveliness for heart and eye,—every charm was hers, from the rosy nails of her tiny feet to the long tresses of her hair that were finer

than silk and dark as night, with blue reflections
in their depths.

Her face with its rich warm complexion, her red
lips, a cup for Love's own drinking, her great eyes
beaming with light and intelligence, promised a com-
pleted beauty of that luxuriant and vigorous type
that reaches perfection only under the burning sun
of the South.

Mansour never wearied of regaling his eyes with
her charms. He admired her as his own *chef
d'œuvre*, as proud of her as if she had been his
own child. He could have filled a book as big as
the Koran, naming and counting and extolling her
charms of person,—the charms he saw, the charms
he had but glimpses of, the hidden charms he
guessed at.

Was it as a father he loved the child,—or as a
lover? He could not tell himself. He was father
and lover in one, the two melting in a single affec-
tion, —pure, strong and uncompromising.

In her presence he became young again; he felt
himself light-hearted and merry. His limbs were
no longer stiff with age, and the rough exterior no
longer visible,—the time-worn case that held a heart
still green and youthful.

All the charms of all his mistresses were summed up
in her. Only she was fairer than all, joining in her
own person the several beauties that had adorned one
or another of his former loves and had separately
enchained his heart. Like *Fathma*, she had long

silken locks that fell in dazzling and iridescent
waves far below her waist; like *Meryem*, the first
Meryem, eyes flashing with the gleam of a drawn
sword in the sun. She possessed the fairy foot of
Embarka the maid of the Sahara, the rounded shape
and virginal form of the second *Meryem*, *Yamina's*
high-arched nose. Her teeth flashed with the
pearly whiteness of *Mabrouka's*, while the clean-cut
delicate limbs recalled *Aïcha* to his mind, the danc-
ing-girl the young men of Biskara call *the Divine*.

That atmosphere of love, the aureole that surrounds
some women, was hers too,—all those mysterious
scents they exhale, coming one knows not whence,
from their hair, from their bosom, from the folds of
their dress, an intoxicating union of perfumes, of
rose and violet, milk and spikenard, frankincense
and musk, lily and jasmine, earth and heaven, the
keen savour of the brunette, delicious and heady,
the soft, voluptuous odour of the blonde, perfumes
of love and woman that mingle with your dreams
and stir you so strangely when you wake.

All this *the Happy Man* enjoyed, drinking in the
savour of her loveliness as a man tries the *bouquet*
of a delicious fruit before venturing to bite into it.
Heart and brain were alike intoxicated; still he
never suffered anything to show on the surface, for
fear of scaring the child's natural modesty. Knowing
vice and all its ways so intimately, he never sus-
pected what was yet the fact, that nothing could
scare her in her absolute innocence.

With her before him, he forgot the blasphemies he had so often repeated in former times, when *blasé* and glutted with self-indulgence, he had afforded matter by his scandalous amours for the whispered colloquies of the women of the tribes. In those days he would say:

"Woman is the daughter of the devil; the inventress of all wickedness!"

"Woman is the mother of deceit; falsehood issued from her mouth, and corruption from her loins!"

"The purest of them leaves behind her a wounded heart, a polluted body!"

"Fools to seek a perfect wife! Why! the Prophet himself, counting women from Eve our Mother, found but four perfect." *

Now he said, as he watched over the child's slumbers:

"Woman is an angel; she brings joy and happiness and life itself!"

VI.

AMID the fresh greenery of her garden a whole legion of merry, noisy birds twittered. Their clamour awoke her soon as ever the sun threw his first rays athwart the gilded bars of her casement.

* The names of the four women Mohammed judged to be perfect are these; Asia, wife of Pharaoh; Mary, mother of Jesus; Khadidja, his first wife; and Fathma, his daughter, who was married to Ali.

In an instant she was up and in the garden. There she washed in the brook under the shade of two or three poplars Mansour had planted when she was an infant, but which now stretched their boughs right over the roof of the *haouch*.

Under their shelter she could lay aside her veil, and bathe in security, for hidden as she was by the leaves, between the house and the thick cactus-hedge, in the close entanglement of lilies, roses and jasmine, no indiscreet eye could possibly spy upon her.

Moreover now that she was grown big, Mansour respected her little maiden secrets, and during her toilette, the *Oudou-el-Kebir* (the Great Preparation) the Prophet has ordained as a piece of religious ritual,— for he well knew how cleanliness of body and cleanliness of mind go together, and how when the bath is neglected, the soul is as foul as the skin,— and equally during the " great ablution," when standing naked and radiant in her young loveliness, she poured the refreshing streams of water over her shoulders and bosom, her hips and every part of her firm young body, he never ventured so much as a glance. His fear of being surprised by her was too great, and the dread of an evil thought entering her maiden heart to pollute it.

So he left her to herself, fully respecting her girlish modesty, but keeping at the same time careful guard out of doors, confident of finding her when the day he longed for had at length arrived, still stainless in all the glow of her pure and sweet maidenhood.

VII.

AFTER the bath, when she returned to the house wrapped in her linen *haïk*, he loved to watch her further toilette.

Now he would make her don the *piquant* costume of the Moorish ladies of *El-Badhadja* the warlike; * now the dress of the girls of the Souf. At another time he would clothe her like the maids of Constantine with the *foutah* (shawl-girdle) drawn tight over the hips or in the ample folds of the *gandourah* falling to the heels. But what delighted him most was to see her wearing the simple tunic the Nomad tribes of the Tell use, open at the sides, leaving the arms bare to the shoulders and fastened there with silver buckles, and clothed as lightly as a girl can be, going to and fro in the house intent on her domestic tasks.

He knew that idleness is mother of evil thoughts, and desired within the narrow circle of their lives to leave no hour unoccupied.

She was still quite small when he began her education, installing among her attendants girls from the tents and girls from the *Hadars*, first one then another, who under his supervision which never relaxed for a moment, taught the child how to cut out and make up the *gandourah*, how to

* Algiers.

weave *haiks*, and how to embroider on white linen
brilliant patterns in silk. She learned too the way
to prepare savoury *couscous* in the great wooden
platter perforated with holes, that rests over the
copper in which whole quarters of meat stew, fla-
vouring it with pimento, and adding hard-boiled
eggs and the breasts of fowls to the mess, and the
art of making honey-cakes, kneading barley-bread,
and compounding conserve of dates.

Moreover she learned to sing the ballads of the
douars, accompanying herself on the resonant
tarbouka. But Mansour had strictly forbidden all
love-ditties; war-songs and the mournful lament
over the loss of Algiers the Beautiful made up her
répertoire. Sung with her childish lips and soft
young voice, these warlike strains had an indescrib-
able charm.

But at her lessons he was always present. He
guarded her like a duenna, and suffered no mention
to be made of matters out of doors. One day a
tofla (young girl) of the *Beni-Mozab*, who was
instructing her in the art of overlaying linen with
threads of gold and silk, happened to hum in her
hearing a catch well-known in the *douars*:

> I wait for my beloved!
> His look is proud and full of love.
> And when I hear his voice,
> Or the sound of his footfall,
> Or the neigh of his charger,
> I know them among a thousand;
> And I feel like to die!

" To die! why to die?" Afsia asked; "why to die, when she is expecting her lover?"

The Mozabite was amused at her naïveté and began to laugh; but Mansour was angry and gave the indiscreet woman no time to reply.

" Begone!" he cried, "begone! you pollute her virtue. Go join him; he is waiting for you. Hark! he is impatient; I hear his bray from the marsh. There's the mate for you!"

Brought up thus aloof from other women, and carefully guarded against contact with other children, —too often an agent of corruption, she remained so pure that the first time she overheard Mansour boasting of her virginity to the men of Djenarah, she asked him what a virgin was.

" A maiden that no evil thought has ever so much as touched," he answered.

" Have the women of Djenarah then all of them evil thoughts, that you told the townsmen their daughters and their sisters were not virgins? What *is* an evil thought?"

" One you cannot avow without blushing?"

" Then I have none," the girl exclaimed; "I am really and truly a virgin."

VIII.

HE smiled at her words. This was indeed the bride he had dreamed of, the fair, gentle girl, pure as the cup of the lily just opened to meet the first kiss of dawn, unsullied as the *Selsebil*, the fountain of Paradise.

And how he guarded the lovely bud that was bursting for him and him alone! What watchfulness and care he lavished on his flower! He recalled all his own experience won in former intrigues that taught all the intricacies of cause and effect in love; and weighed each *if* and *but*, every *why* and *wherefore!* Old jackal, he had so often prowled round his neighbours' farmyard, that he knew both how to steal and how to keep a thief at bay, and it must be a wise man to teach him anything new. Daughters of Fathma, your wiles are beyond compare, but his vigilance too was beyond compare, and his astuteness and the precautions he adopted.

His *haouch*, as I mentioned, stood far from any road, on purpose to prevent as far as might be unexpected and unwished for visits or the arrival of importunate wayfarers who think all they have to do to claim a right to hospitality is to come shouting before your door, "All hail, Master; lo! here am I, a guest of God." He had contrived to put the marsh between himself and the main-road, and it was needful to follow a series of little winding paths half-hid among the rushes and make a considerable detour to reach his dwelling.

Nevertheless, when it *did* happen that a benighted traveller or passing beggar came to his door, hungry, thirsty and tired, he was ready with his, "Welcome, stranger!"

He put a good face on it, and received him as a Musulman is bound to receive his guests, for has not our Prophet written:

"Blessed is he and pious who shares his board and his bed with the orphan, the poor man, the traveller, yea! with all that have need thereof. Him shall God guard from all ill that may fall from heaven above or spring from the earth beneath." And again. "Be ye of loving-kindness towards your guest; for the same, entering your gates, bringeth a blessing along with him, and departing, taketh away your offences." And again, "God will do no hurt to the hand which hath given an alms," as is written in the chapter that is called *The Cow.*

He silenced the dogs, and held the stranger's stirrup to help him dismount; or if he were on foot and weary, took him by the arm and led him to a seat.

On such a day he had a great fire lighted, the quarter of a sheep roasted and two fowls killed, that the guest might be refreshed and say at parting. "I have a full belly."

Afsia never showed herself on these occasions, but she made a honey-cake for the stranger and sent it him by a servant.

When the guest had dined, and lay down to sleep by the dying embers of the fire on a couch of the thick-wooled white fleeces of the sheep of the Upper Tell, Mansour stretched himself on a

mat of *alpha*-grass across the door guarding the
stone staircase that led to the young girl's sleeping-
chamber, and never closed an eye till dawn.

Then without asking name or rank, without asking
whence the stranger came nor were he was going,
he brought him his beast ready saddled and well
fed like his master, or if he possessed neither horse
nor mare nor mule, his staff and scrip, the latter
well lined by Afsia's care, and said:

"Go, and my blessing go with you!"

But such visits were rare. The town was near
enough to rob the traveller of the wish to turn out
of his way in order to knock at the door of the
lonely *haouch*. Besides, the name of the Caïd, his
brother, the nobility of his family, the fame ˙that
yet lingered of his former prowess, and more than
all, the suspicion of madness that brooded over
this strange lonely man, made him too much feared
and respected for any to try to take advantage
of him.

IX.

MEANTIME Afsia was approaching womanhood, a
brilliant star rising in the firmament of life, but *he*
was growing bent with years and verging nearer
his setting. Children press their elders down the
steep hill of age; we see their bloom, and realize
that our own is departing; as our sap fails, theirs
is rising higher and higher. When *they* flower, it

means that *we* shall soon be but the withered fruit on a dead tree.

Youth on one side, age on the other,—an abyss was opening between, though neither he nor she measured its full depth. *He* felt his heart still green, and failed to see his body was out-worn; *she* in her ignorance and inexperience, knew not as yet she had a heart, and the claims nature rouses in the bodies of the young were as yet unheard.

Loving and beloved, she grew like a tender plant in the peace of her home, and dreamed of no other existence.

House, garden, poplars fringing the fountain, the marsh and its rushes, with mists floating over it at dawn and a light curtain of fog at evening, the wide grey plain, and beyond, the gently swelling blue hills,—this was her country, her horizon, her world.

There she lived her life, and wished for no change.

At times she would gaze dreamily towards the town, striving to make out its old crumbling walls where they rose amid the tangled vegetation of the oasis; but all she could see was the gay carpet of greenery from which the slender minaret of the mosque sprang gracefully into the air.

She felt a secret terror of the mass of houses yonder, the coming and going of so many people and animals, the men and women who seemed, as she passed by on her mule folded in Mansour's arms, to be trying to pierce her veil with their eyes and stare her out of countenance.

How could people live and breathe mid this accumulation of stone and mortar, where many breaths intermingled and the air seemed to stifle the lungs! Ah! how much better it was in the lonely *haouch* where she was free to move and free to breathe in her spacious room!

There she dwelt, and sang songs in her heart that she had never read in any book written by man, nor learned from any tongue of woman, songs the deep voice of the Autumn winds whispered in her ear, as they careered over the plains, bending low the reeds in the marsh and tossing the *burnouses* of the horsemen that galloped afar, stooping over the necks of their flying steeds.

Or again, when the sky was gloomy with red and yellow storm-clouds she would hear the coming of the *Simoom*, and with eyes that were faint with a strange delight and dilated nostrils, run to meet its fiery kiss.

Symptoms such as these alarmed Mansour, and he cried:

"Why do you so? the *Simoom*-wind bites, and its bite is fatal to young maids."

"No! it does not bite," she replied, "its breath is a kiss, and I love to feel it."

At other times she was pensive yet alert, seeming to await she knew not what. She would smile a vague smile, dreaming perchance of that unknown something that springs up of a sudden in our path, and shapes the destiny of our life.

" What are you dreaming of?" the old man asked; and she would answer him:

" Yonder I hear the song of the birds. I listen to the voice of the quail calling her mate in the barley-fields. You who know everything, tell me what it is she says."

X.

In her great dark eyes was clearly reflected a soul filled with wonderment, vague and impalpable. Her thoughts still all indeterminate floated on the mists of ignorance and inexperience, while her sentiments, or rather her sensations, could not and dared not unfold their buds and blossom forth beside a man like Mansour, in whom the terrible strength of his passions had induced a premature maturity, or over-maturity of body.

Old men's love is a fire that gives off no heat. They diffuse around them an atmosphere of chill constraint that freezes and paralyzes the heart. Children reared by the old grow up sickly like plants condemned to 'the shade. Age is wintry, whereas the young need heat to make them blossom, and sun and free air.

Like those flowers that close their petals at the approach of cold, Afsia shut herself up in her bright childish dreams, building up in her young heart a brilliant shrine for Love to dwell in, vaguely and intuitively conscious of his nature, as girls are though they may be ignorant of his very name.

Sometimes could be distinguished the long line of a caravan in the distance making its way across the plains. Then she would follow it with long looks, especially marking the high-perched palanquins wherein the daughters of these Nomad wanderers rode secluded, and sighing to think of their ampler lives who thus travelled the wide world.

The blood of the Sahara that throbbed in her veins, told her there were vast horizons, unbroken and unbounded, beyond the hills. Thither her thoughts flew, and she longed to follow them to this far land.

But the *Thaleb* was on the watch, and never failed to say to her:

"Foolish! foolish! who find the peace and security you enjoy dull and wearisome. How can you envy yonder women? Scorched by burning sun or lashed by storms that sweep from the wind-reddened horizon, with parched throats and eyes smarting from the sand, they follow involuntarily the fated fortunes of father or husband. Their life is a never-ending struggle; they travel on and on, bread so hard to win and thirst so easy, and covet the lot of the shepherd lad sitting by the wayside and watching the train go by. Day after day for many a day they long for the happiness that lies ready to your hand every hour, but which you care not to enjoy."

"Happiness! what happiness?" asked Afsia.

"Shade, rest, and a stream of cool, fresh water."

To this she could not find a word to answer.
She had never felt hunger or thirst. She possessed
a shelter against days that were too hot and nights
too damp; she knew nothing of the pain of weari-
ness and the shuddering horror of anticipation on
the approach of danger. But she told herself this
could never be the be all and end all of existence,
—mere dull comfort of body, mere enjoyment of
peace and quietness; she felt that beyond all this,
there might indeed be suffering, there might be
peril, but there *must* be a wider life and ampler joys.

XI.

SHE loved too to follow with her eyes the horse-
men of the *goums* with their great straw hats
plumed with black ostrich feathers, as they sped
across the plain in admired disorder. She could
distinguish by their scarlet *burnouses* the Caïd and
Sheikhs in the van, and the blue robes of the *Mok-
alis*; then the rest, all in white, long gun on thigh,
following in close ordered ranks. Some galloped
on the flanks of the company, their horses' feet
raising clouds of yellow dust. She wondered at
the trailing horse-coverings of silk that floated on
the wind, the flashing arms, the green standards
with the silver crescent; she listened to the gay
beat of the *tam-tam*, the shrill notes of the fife,
and the crash of the muskets; and seemed to
behold a procession out of fairyland passing before
her eyes wrapped in a golden cloud.

But what she liked best was the ordered lines of red-coated horsemen that twice or thrice in the year filed across the grey plain. They rode two and two in serried ranks. They had no silken horse-coverings, no ostrich plumes; they were all clad alike in white and red and blue. A sword with scabbard of steel passed under the left thigh and showed up against the black felt of the saddle, and on their backs the brass and steel mountings of their muskets flashed in the sun.

It was a squadron of the Spahis of Constantine, on their way to the advanced post of *Zery-bet-el-Oued* to relieve garrison.

Long she watched them, with beating heart and pensive eyes, listening eagerly as though to catch the rattle of sword-blades in their scabbards and the jingle of spurs and stirrups.

It is always thus; woman loves the sword, that terrifies her. Weak and tender being, she is irresistibly drawn by force of contrast to admire the murderous crash of arms. Her heart bows before the *shedder of blood*.

Afsia longed that the road had been nearer the *haouch*, that she might have looked into the bold faces of the soldiers.

She remembered how once, when she was younger and was returning from Djenarah seated on Mansour's mule, they had met the red horsemen, and one of them had said:

"Well met! Look, my children, see the bride of

El-Messaoud. You can only see her great eyes;
but they shine like two stars, and are sweet as a
spring in the desert. With such a blessing on
your saddle, none need wonder men call you *the
Happy Man!*"

The Spahis fixed their eyes on her with delight,
and as they passed, greeted Mansour one after the
other:

"All hail, Mansour! the Prophet wrap your *tofla*
round with blessings as with a garment!"

"A blessing be on you and yours!" he returned,
proud and happy.

Then they continued their march in silence. But
in every group of men, there are always a few
ready to sow hate and discord; so when they were
a short distance away, one of these ill-natured in-
dividuals turned in his saddle and shouted back:

"Ho! Happy Man! keep you your rose-bud, till
it opens; then we will come and pluck it."

All set up a laugh at this; and Mansour, trem-
bling with rage, cried back:

"My flower is not for you, you son of a dog,
that serve the unbelieving dogs!"

Then the rest, stung by the insult, replied:

"We will rob the treasure; we will rob the fair
bride's treasure. It is not for an old goat like
him!"

Afsia understood nothing of this scene, and longed
to know what it was they threatened to rob her of;
but Mansour was so angry she dared not question

him.   Later on she asked him about it, but he
roughly bade her be silent.

It was the first and only time he had ever spoken
roughly to her; so all the more vividly, when she
saw the red horsemen pass by in the distance, she
recalled the admiration their looks had expressed,
the flattering words they had said of her, Mansour's
anger, and their mocking threat.

XII.

THEN without rhyme or reason a feeling of sadness
would come over her; and Mansour would try to
amuse her with some wondrous Eastern tale, care-
fully omitting the only part of it she cared to hear,
the tender love-adventures of hero and heroine.

So while she listened with one ear to the *Thaleb's*
voice, the other was striving to catch the soft mys-
terious murmur that had for some time past been
ever whispering in her heart.   It seemed to come
from some far off, unknown clime, that neither her
black nurse from the Soudan, nor yet Mansour,
who knew so much, had ever told her of in their
stories of *genii*, magicians and enchanted palaces.

She would shut her eyes, sheltering her secret
thoughts under the veil of their lids, and listen to
the old man's tales—without really hearing one word
he said.

A nervous spasm traversed her limbs, she stretched
herself with arms above her head, as if she felt

sleep coming on her, and filled with a great lassitude would remain for hours, motionless in a kind of depression, dreaming with eyes open, letting time slip by unheeded. Then towards evening, when the breeze from the north blew sharply on her arms and shoulders, running lovingly along her bare limbs, lashing her as with light blows of a whip, she received its caress with delight, and shook off the torpor that had oppressed her during the day. She felt a strange warmth and excitement glide into her veins and sighed.

" What are you thinking of?" said Mansour.

But she answered, blushing as if she had been detected in a fault:

" Nothing at all. Only ideas that wander in my head, and lead I don't know where to."

So saying, she ran away into her little garden, and bending low over her flowers, plunged her gaze to the bottom of their calyx, as though to discover the mysterious wonders lurking within; dazzled by the brilliant colours, intoxicated by the sweet scents, the girl longed to be one of the little blue flies she saw fluttering round, to slip into these miniature palaces, more splendid than those the *Thaleb* told her the fairy marvels of.

" Enough! Enough! I can see within my flowers what is more beautiful than all you tell me about."

XIII.

HE had fixed fourteen years as the age at which
he meant to take her as his wife; this epoch he
had determined to wait for in order that the girl
might be fully formed and give him vigorous sons.
Some amongst us take their wives at twelve years
old. This is wrong. A woman forced into marriage
prematurely fades early, and bears only puny, sickly
offspring. Such children show all their life long
pallid faces and weakling bodies inherited from their
mother, while their spirit is like untempered metal
that loses its edge as soon as ever it meets the
rough realities of life.

The Prophet says: " Fix not the bands of matri-
mony before the fit time shall be accomplished."

He does not *prescribe* the fit time, but leaves it
to the wise discretion of mankind. Besides, mothers
and matrons, whose task it is to find the meet
bride, have quick eyes to see whether the bud is
opened. They possess more skill than we to mark
the precise moment when the rose is not indeed
full-blown as yet, but at the same time no longer
a bud. This is the delicious moment at which to
take our wife, and for this moment Mansour was
waiting.

There were still some weeks to run ere she
reached the appointed age; meanwhile he watched
the development of her virgin beauty with admira-

tion and delight, loving her at once as a father and as a lover. The latter love was perhaps still vague and indeterminate, shrinking before the stern austerity of the other.

Undoubtedly if she had been a stranger to him, if he had not day by day been a delighted spectator of 'the budding of ever new and unexpected charms of maiden loveliness, his passions, still unexhausted by all his excesses, would have awakened with their old fire and fury unabated; but having sheltered her in his arms like a bird flying for refuge to its mother's wing, reared and watched over her like a nestling of his own, heard her soft voice greet him each morn at her waking with the dear name of father, that sounded like a kiss uttered by her smiling lips, the old debauchee who had corrupted so many others in his time, would have looked upon it as sacrilege to assail her innocence.

The idea of anticipating the marriage day never crossed his mind but as a piece of impossible wickedness; nay! sometimes he asked himself whether, when the rite *had* been celebrated, very shame would not deter him from taking her to his couch. He blushed at the thought of soiling with wanton kisses, battered greybeard that he was, the pure lips of the lovely child.

At times when she lay asleep, he would draw near noiselessly, and watching her budding breasts lift as she lightly breathed, would silently drink in the delight of her virgin charms. But it was rather the self-conscious pride an artist feels in the work of art he has created than a lover's eager longing to possess.

"Yes! she is mine," he would say. "I have brought her up, cherished her, watched her grow. I have been father and mother to her, brother and sister, master and friend. I have shared her earliest gambols, and wiped away her first tears. All she knows, I have taught her; the unsullied thoughts that stir in her brain, I have instilled them. I have shut the door against evil influences. To me she owes her beauty, her health and strength; for I have let her develop untrammelled and unstinted like a flower of the fields; I have given as companions, her only comrades, the sky and its clouds and stars, the mountains and the plains, and liberty. She is mine, mine only, and she knows it well. She knows she is my very own, from her raven locks to her rosy feet.

Then he would take her tiny feet in his long rugged hands of bronze, and with bent head as though in prayer, would imprint a kiss on them.

Once or twice the child awoke with his hot breath on her cheeks, and seeing him kneeling at her bedside, half opened her lips to smile at him, then closing her lids again, went back to her dreams of fairyland.

XIV.

ONE morning Mansour said to her:

"Afsia, the great day, the day of blessing, draws near. When fifteen times you shall have seen the sun set from to-day, you will enter your fifteenth year. 'Tis the age I have for fourteen years been waiting for. I have waited with patience, for each day added a fresh petal to the flower of your beauty. Now it is complete and perfect. The bud uncloses, the moment to pluck it is come. Afsia, I would tell you a secret, one that for fourteen years has been the great secret of my heart. I buried it deep in my bosom, that it might not throw a shadow over the white purity of your soul. Now I reveal it. My youth, Afsia, has gone, like the water of a spring the *Simoom* has dried up, leaving but the bare stones of its bed that resemble a skeleton; but I trust to you, unsullied fountain of my heart, to fill the dried up watercourse again and refresh its thirsty banks. Afsia, sweet song of my life, I trust to your smile to bring back to my old heart, worn and chilled by winter, all the gay sunbeams of spring. Afsia, tell me, have I done well?"

"Father, I hardly understand your meaning. But if your heart has trusted to mine and your will relied on my obedience, you *have* done well in both."

"I thank you, my child. I will explain my words.

He whom the men of the Tell have entitled *Thaleb*, and they of the Beled-el-Djerid *Messaoud*, he whom all call *Sidi-el-Hadj*, Mansour-ben-Ahmed himself, is about to give you the name of wife.... Afsia, does the prospect please you, are you willing?"

"Your wife!" she cried in amazement; "but how can that be, when I am your daughter?"

"You are my *adopted* daughter, Afsia. No tie of blood connects us. There is no obstacle; you may become flesh of my flesh, the vesture of my life, the fruitful seed-field where I must plant my vine,—no obstacle, if you are willing. I ask you *are* you willing?"

"Your words are still dark to me, Mansour. Doubtless I am dull of understanding. I am not all-wise like you. But see, if it is your wish I cease to be your daughter and become your wife, I am indeed willing. But why wait for fifteen days? As you appear to desire it so eagerly, why cannot you marry me to-day?"

"Ah! soul of my life; can it be you desire it so ardently,—is your love as great as mine?"

"Love?"

"Yes! can it be you feel your heart stirred for my old grey beard?"

"Why, yes! I love you. Are you not my father, and my mother, and all I have?"

"But it is not so a husband would be loved; he must be loved as a lover."

"As a lover?.... Ah, well! you shall teach me

how I am to love you. I will do it as you will, and I desire what you wish."

He took her hands and kissed them.

"White blossom of the plain!" he cried in a transport of joy, "whose eyes are gentle as the heifers' that roam the Tell, whose looks are a song of love, flower of womanhood, *houri* and angel, I will instruct you what you must do. But govern your impatience; the day, the thrice-happy day, will be here anon."

XV.

AFSIA remained long in thought. Never, never had she dreamed a thing so extraordinary. To be Mansour's bride!—a man standing at the gates of old age, while she,—she was just on the threshold of life! It seemed a very strange thing to her; but her thoughts did not go beyond.

The word *bride* that exercises many young heads so, had no meaning for her. She asked herself what great difference it would make in her life, to be called wife instead of daughter of the *Thaleb*.

At the bottom of her heart, warm and ready as it was to expand before the fire of tenderness, was no desire and no regret, no repulsion and no fear. "I sadly want experience to become his wife," she thought, "but he is good, and he will teach me my duties." So she accepted her new part simply because such was Mansour's wish, because such

acceptance seemed to please him, just as she would
have been ready at his pleasure to change her robe
or unbind her hair.

Afsia felt none of that vague trouble of mind the
city girl experiences, who is never altogether un-
informed, for all her mother has done to maintain
as long as possible her maiden innocence of mind
and body,—an innocence the husband will one day
dissipate so suddenly and so roughly.

Neither did she feel the amorous longing and
delight of the country girl, who witnessing daily
as she must the pairing of the beasts of the field,
can never, however chaste in body, be chaste in
thought, when she enters the husband's bed.

She was as ignorant to-day of the mysterious
processes whereby the human race is perpetuated
as the hour when the *Thaleb* took her fresh from
her mother's womb and bore her away wrapped in
a *haïk*.

Thus on the eve of the great epoch so momentous
to women, never a one of those lascivious *djinns*
that make maids feel faint with wanton thoughts
and their bosom shudder with tremblings of desire,
had ever visited her at night time; and when her
spirit wandered to the land of dreams, the angel
Asraël might have followed her there.

And Mansour, happy and on the point of attain-
ing his wish, could boast:

" She is virgin, the pearl of Djenarah; her clear
eye is like almsgiving, it shuts the doors of evil...

She is virgin, Sidi-Messaoud's bride,—as pure as
the spring that wells from the rock, as pure as her
own thoughts.   I swear it,

By God all-powerful;

By the head of the Prophet of God;

By the oath of Abraham, the friend of God;

By the Koran, the Book of Truth;

No other man but I has seen her face; no hardy
look has ever offended her modesty! "

XVI.

MANSOUR decided that the wedding should take
place at the town, where henceforth he proposed
to live.   His time of waiting and trial was over.
The dear child had refashioned his soul and cleansed
it of every stain of the past.   A new life was to
begin, from now.

Old men are as confident as young; they form
projects, seeming to think all the time they have
left behind is still before them.   Some pile up a
hoard of silver, others build costly houses, others
again plant young palm-trees.   Do not imagine
they do it for their sons! they say so, but they
don't believe it in their secret hearts.   They are
working for themselves, they are still eager to enjoy.
They do not see that Death walks by their side,
with arm uplifted to strike; and that at the very
moment they stretch out their hand to grasp the
fruit they covet and have ripened with such pains,
he will close their mouth for ever.

Mansour had sworn to himself and before witnesses to marry a virgin. Now his end is all but attained: yet probably after a few days' enjoyment of the prize, when his first desires have been satisfied, he will set about the pursuit of some other object.

He had bought by his brother's agency a house worthy of the pearl he would enshrine in it, a house with garden and interior courtyard and orange trees that filled the whole abode with their perfume. The door of massive oak felled in the forests of the Eastern Khabyles, was studded with huge nails made by the ironworkers in the forges of Flissa.

A single window gave on the street, and this he intended to have walled up the very day after his marriage.

Henceforth sure of his treasure, and having no longer the hard task of guarding a maiden's virtue, but only the easier care of a good and submissive wife, he could begin life again on the old lines! So he thought, foolish man! but we indulge in dreams to the last hour of existence,—and we do well, for it is dreams that clothe the dry bones of life. Alas! for the fool who in his fancied wisdom roughly tears down the delicate, light veil. By doing so, he strips away the sole cloak that prevents our feeling the bitter tooth of time.

XVII.

HE would give a marriage-feast that should long be remembered. All the town should be invited; a hundred sheep, twenty loads of *couscous*, twenty loads of dates, should be provided. Young and old, rich and poor, village-folk and townsfolk, strangers and sojourners, all should share the banquet. Every gun should be fired in his honour, and the Caïd should supply the powder.

In Allah's name! men should tell of it years hence in the *Ksours*, and in the *Beled-el-Djerid*, and in the Tell. There were still old men living, connected with his former days, men whose wives he had stolen from them, whose sisters and daughters he had won over, and these above all others he was eager to see seated at his table.

They were ignorant of their shame, or pretended to be so; but if they *had* suspicions, they could retaliate with their sarcasms,—in this way avenging the wrong, of all wrongs the one that bites deepest, which the villain had cast on them on his passage, as an old spiteful witch casts the evil eye on her neighbours.

These were his *bosom-enemies*; for had he not searched their bosoms to the quick to sow his deadly seed there? But far from dreading them, the old champion had fearlessly left them alone for fourteen long years to whet their venomous tongues on him.

For them he was no *Thaleb*, neither Mansour the happy, nor Mansour the brave,—but the *mad* Mansour.

Yet others there were to push their abominable spite further still. These asserted that the aged libertine had taken little Afsia only in order to better pollute her at his will and pleasure, at that tender age when a child has not yet lost her first teeth. They said he could not hide her away so completely, but that you could discover in her faded cheek signs of precocious vice.

In a word, men had so mocked him, had so vilified him with calumny, that now he longed to crown his triumph with every circumstance of brilliancy and renown.

XVIII.

HE was to take up his abode at Djenarah eight days before the wedding. In this he had yielded to a caprice of the child's who was eager and inquisitive to see her new home; besides, he required to superintend the final preparations. As of old, he seated her before him on his mule, wrapping her more carefully than ever in his *haïk*, so as to show only the deep, black line of her great eyes.

The little country girl, who knew only her own

haouch of common stone and plaster, was entranced
with the magnificence of the new home, that was
fit to be the *harem* of a *Bach-Agha*. All the
splendour of Arab luxury, imported at great cost
from the bazaars of Tunis and Constantine, dis-
played its flashing colours and sparkling surfaces.

The rich merchant of former days willingly ex-
pended a part of his fortune on these pomps. It
was to enshrine his idol! what better investment
could he have?

In your country, I have heard say, old debauchees
and men of pleasure do the same for courtesans
possessing neither youth nor beauty; but the Mus-
sulman surpasses the Christian a hundred-fold.

He proceeded to present her future attendants
to her: three girls from the country of the *Souab*
and the negress who had been her nurse and who,
laughing and crying at one and the same time,
kissed her beautiful mistress's hands and feet. Then
he showed her the chamber made ready to receive
the bride. It opened on the gallery of the first
floor, already scented with the perfumes they use
in the seraglio. Her tiny feet disappeared in the
thick rich carpets of Tunis, and sitting down she
was buried amid bright-hued silken cushions. Tall
lilies in pots of red and blue earthenware held
their graceful heads aloft, while at the little window
with its gilt bars, festoons of oasis-flowers fell
sweeping to the ground.

At this window, after the wedding-night, a matron

must—so custom ordains,—show to the impatient crowd on the extended sheet the triumphant irrefutable proof of her virginity.

XIX.

Now just as they were entering the town by the Biskara gate, a horseman wearing the red *burnouse* of the Spahis met them. He was riding down the middle of the street, mounted on a bare-backed horse which he was taking to water at the rivulet that irrigates the gardens. At this spot the way is narrow, an arrangement that makes defence the easier in the event of a hostile attack, and the terraced houses, low and closely crowded together, barely allow three horsemen to pass side by side. Accordingly the *Thaleb* drew his mule a little on one side, and as the other passed, their looks met. What he saw made the *Thaleb* thoughtful, while the Spahi on the contrary went on his way unheeding. But as he was sallying from the lofty archway of the towered gate, he heard voices saying:

"Look! friends. Look, there goes Sidi-Messaoud and his future bride!"

These words roused his curiosity, and touching the shoulder of a passer-by whose eyes were fixed on Mansour's retreating form:

"Friend!" said he, "who is yonder Sheikh with the grey beard who defies custom and carries his bride before him on the *berda* of his mule?"

" You are a stranger," replied the basser-by, " else you must know him."

" You have said it, sir! I am a stranger in the town."

" He is well known in the *Beled-el-Djerid* and the south of the Tell, and for fifteen years past he has been much in men's mouths in Djenarah the Pearl. He is brother of the Caïd *Brahim-ben-Ahmed*. His name is Mansour, but they call him *El-Messaoud*, because he succeeds in all he does. Lo! there you see him, the ancient greybeard, guarding the maidenhood of the young girl that is to be his bride."

The horseman smiled:

" Ha! ha! that is a droll tale. There is *no* virginity however closely guarded but escapes at last. Friend! a girl's maidenhood is like a happy day, it's gone, vanished, before you know it has slipped your fingers. The old goat reminds me of the *Chaouch* who long watched about the prison,—long after the prisoner had fled."

" The prisoner is still within," returned the other with a laugh, " if we may believe report; but it won't be so much longer."

" Why? is the wedding near?"

" In a week, my son. The whole town is bidden to it. They tell of a hundred sheep roasted whole! There will be more than three hundred guns. If you have no pressing business, I should stay till then."

" Perhaps I may; 'tis well worth while. Sir! I thank you."

He went on his way to the stream, but he too had now grown thoughtful, and kept saying over to himself:

" Mansour-ben-Ahmed *the Happy Man!* By the head of the Prophet, the name of the man my mother cursed before she died!"

He tarried long under the leafy trees that extend their strong branches over the fresh water, washed down his horse carefully, took him back to the stable and gave him his barley. Then he went and sat at the door of the *caouadji* in the street of Biskara, and bade them bring him a cup of coffee.

Whilst he was drinking it slowly, taking little sips and gazing meanwhile into vacancy, he heard the steps of a mule, and saw Mansour and Afsia quitting the town.

XX.

HE rose instinctively to look closely into the old man's face, but before the piercing, cold eye of Mansour he dropped his own, ashamed to have made a display of ill-bred curiosity, and putting his hand on his heart, he said in a loud voice:

" *Salamalek oum!*"

"On you too be blessing!" returned Mansour, and pursued his way.

Standing in the middle of the street, the Spahi watched him disappear under the long vaulted passage of the gate of the *ksour.* Suddenly a hand was placed familiarly on his shoulder:

" What do you here, Omar?"

His questioner was a man of forty-five, burly and red-faced, clothed in the habit of a wealthy merchant.

" Ah! 'tis you, my host," replied the Spahi, " I am glad to have met you.   Tell me, who and what is yonder good man we see, who carries perched before him on his saddle so incomparably fair a maid."

" His name is Mansour-ben-Ahmed! . . . . . " the other replied slowly, " and they call him further *the Happy Man*."

" And he is guarding the virginity of his future bride.   I learned that much two hours ago; but I could learn no more."

" I will tell you more.   You do right, Omar, to inquire; for it may well be this man's history is bound up with yours, with mine, as it is with that of many in this place.   It may even be this was why I wrote bidding you join me here."

" By the head of my father, who left me to wander through the world like a lost dog, by the blessed head of my mother who died with shame on her brow and a curse on her lips, your words make a strange light to dawn in my head.   Speak, Lagdar, son of El-Arbi, explain your meaning."

Then the merchant took his arm, saying to the Spahi, " Come with me!"

XXI.

A FEW days later the South wind was blowing over the plains, wrapping them in red stifling dust that caught the throat like the powder of the *kari* (red-pepper). Nothing stirred, man and beast had sought shelter from the burning blasts of the *Simoom*. The camels crouching low with outstretched necks breathed noisily, whilst the drivers, their heads buried under the corner of a ragged *burnouse*, cowered under the shade of the higher sand-hills, or lay half suffocated beneath some scanty clump of *chicch* or alpha-grass.

Mansour had made an artificial night in the rooms of the *haouch* by stretching *frechias* over every opening by which light could penetrate. A single ray admitted would have filled the house with blinding light and clouds of mosquitoes. Every window was darkened and every door shut close, while porous vases of water hung swinging by cords and diffused around some of their freshness.

Old man and young girl were sleeping the heavy sleep that comes in the daytime, putting lead on the eyelids and folding the limbs in chains of steel, when suddenly the dogs gave voice to a low savage growling. Mansour awoke and opened the door sharply. The previous day at the same hour they had barked furiously. He remembered the fact, and throwing a look all round, cried in his strong voice:

" Ho! there. If you crave meat or drink, come
and ask it openly, but if you are marauders and
come to prowl round my house, I tell you this,—
you prowl round your death."

He looked and listened long, but he could see
nothing but the she-goat and her kid, returning
from the direction of the marshes of Ain-Chabrou,
and could hear nothing but the howling of the
Simoom.

XXII.

THE glowing coppery tints the East assumes after
the passage of the desert wind reddened the sky
above the faint blue line of the hills, when Afsia
left her chamber.

Her eyes were tired and heavy, and she felt the
dull uncomfortable sensation of having slept too
long. She knelt down languidly on the carpet, and
whilst she arranged before a little copper-framed
mirror her long tresses disordered in sleep, half
asleep still and following out her interrupted dreams,
the *Thaleb* gazed at her smiling.

She caught his look fixed on her and blushed.
Her bosom was bare, and she observed that it was
on it Mansour kept his eyes. Yet many a time
before, without her specially noting the fact, he had
offered the same impalpable caress; but now a feeling
of shame seemed to have attacked her of a sudden,
for she drew her *gandourah* hastily across her

breast, and said with the pouting lips of a spoilt child :

" I do not like you to look at me when I am dressing."

" The husband," returned Mansour, " has the right to look."

" But you are not my husband yet," she put in.

The girl was right, he thought, to remind him of what propriety demanded, and in order to leave her quite undisturbed at her toilette, he went outside and sitting down cast his eagle eye over every quarter of the plain. The world was awaking to life, as it does at the dawn of day, but silently and slowly. The dogs still drowsy were rolling on the sand, and Afsia's pet goat with her kid by her side was browsing on the cactus shoots that pierced the stony soil near the green fence, while in the garden the birds could be heard clapping their tiny wings.

On the horizon the sun was setting in a bath of molten gold. Borne by the breeze came the far-off tones of the Muezzin's voice, calling from the summit of the Mosque of Djenarah to the four quarters of the world :

" Allah Kebir ! Allah Kebir ! " (God is Great).

XXIII.

AT this hour plants exhale their most penetrating odours. Like love-sick maids who, exhausted by the heat of the day and longing at its close to ease their

languid breasts, breathe deep, long-drawn sighs of
relief, the roses, lilies and hyacinths, all the flowers
Afsia loved so well, sent forth a breath that even
reached the *haouch* of the very quintessence of
their scents.

They seemed to be appealing to her senses, and
crying, "Come into the garden, come!" And Afsia,
fresh and free and scented like her flowers, came
forth and seated herself in the midst of her sisters.

There was no regular path, no formal borders or
straight lines or symmetrically ordered flower-beds,
but a luxuriant flood of blossoms and greenery.
The seeds the *Thaleb* had sown were mingled with
others the wind had brought,—who knows from
whence,—all intermixed, intertangled, intermarried.
Nature, all-powerful and inimitable artist, filled this
little corner of virgin soil with the magic creations
of her fancy.

Afsia, as I said, came hither to rest, and her
thoughts floating on the golden clouds of evening
were fain to fly far away into the blue distance of
the heavens.

Buried amid her flowers, her senses stirred by their
perfumes and intoxicated by their brilliant colours,
she listened to the rivulet prattling on its way, to
the murmur of insects and the song of birds. She
lay down, her limbs extended beneath the leaves
of the bananas, her eyes swimming in an ecstasy,
and dreamed of the gardens the Prophet promises
to the elect and of herself a *houri* in their glades.

Presently, as it happened, the kid came gambolling to her and its mother swept her face caressingly with her pointed beard. It was the milking hour, and she cried to the Thaleb to throw her a *settla* that she might fill it with goat's milk.

She passed her fingers under the long, swollen teats, pushing and pulling with gentle rhythmical touches the warm distended udder. Then suddenly she uttered an exclamation of surprise.

"What is it?" asked Mansour, where he sat on the threshold of the *haouch* telling over the beads of his ivory rosary.

She pondered a moment, then replied:

"Nothing .... only that Maaza trod on my foot."

But Maaza, standing quite quiet and placid, had done nothing of the sort. The docile beast was waiting patiently for her young mistress to resume milking, while the maid of the *haouch*, quiet also outwardly but with beating heart, had just told the first falsehood of her life.

XXIV.

THE falsehood had sprung to her lips by a sort of instinct, without her knowing why she told it, and though no one had ever taught her deceit. She lied, because she was weak and a woman, and lying is the natural resource of the weak.

Attached to the goat's horns, half hidden in the white tufts of her coat, was a tiny scrap of cardboard, no longer than a baby's finger, hanging by a silk thread, and on it the one word written:

" *Naabek!*—I love thee."

At the first moment she had uttered a cry of surprise, but reading the magic word, had thought better of it and invented her falsehood. Love! it must be something wrong, else why this secrecy in declaring it? but as it was wrong, then she too must be secret.

And she called to mind a question she had once asked the *Thaleb*, which he had not answered, though he knew everything:

" What *is* love?"

But at the word " I love thee," all the woman awoke in her.

Concealing the charm between her breasts, she rose with affected unconcern and went and offered the *settla* full of milk to Mansour. But seized with a sudden agitation she could not help casting sundry furtive glances of fear and saying to herself that somewhere near, hidden among the cactuses of the garden or the reeds of the marsh, a strange man was watching her. The feeling was so strong as to be actually painful, and the girl put her hand to her heart, that was beating a gallop in her childish bosom.

If she had had her *haïk* with her, she would have drawn it over her face, she felt so keenly the pollution, as it were, of the inquisitive gaze fixed upon her. Her agitation would not have escaped a mother's attention, but a father, even a lover, had no eyes for it, and Mansour saw nothing.

She was afraid to return to the garden, and ran for refuge to her own room; she longed to be alone to hearken to the secrets the beating of her heart told her.

She was at once surprised, agitated and delighted, terrified and pleased.

Who could he be? where was he hiding? Was he young? Was he the son of an Emir or of a Bach-Agha? How came he to love her? Where had he seen her? How had he managed to fasten the charm to the goat's horns?

She looked out fearfully from her little barred window towards the marshes of *Ain-Chabrou*, eager and anxious and afraid, expecting every moment to see a man's head rise suddenly above the rushes.

Long she gazed, till night was fully fallen, but she saw nothing but the long line of dark reeds sharply defined against the grey of the plain in the dying light of the setting sun.

XXV.

NEXT day, at the hour when all the land is bathed in the gentle brilliancy of the dawn and the tufted grasses on the hill-sides tremble at the first kiss of the morning breeze, when the lark rises singing into the crystal sky, Omar the Spahi slipped silently through the reeds of the marsh of *Ain-Chabrou*.

He waited long. He possessed patience, which is better than using force, and that stubbornness that spells success. He was a man rich in resource. If a way were barred, he knew how to find a loophole in the barricade; if he met an obstacle, he did not say, "Stop, there's something in the way," nor did he say, "An obstacle, oh! jump over it." He said nothing, but he slipped round it.

From earliest boyhood he had come into collision with men, and he still bore the bruises of these collisions. As he grew older, he said, "It is my turn to bruise others." No one knew his father, but he was called Omar; yet when he came to Dar-el-Bey to enlist in the squadron of Spahis of Constantine, he presented a valuable horse of the stock of the Bou-Ghareb and excellent certificates from the Native Department. Accordingly he had been enrolled on the spot, and when the sergeant who was entering his name asked him, "Yes! Omar, —son of whom?" he answered loftily: "*Bou-Skin*,"—father of the sword.

The clerks all raised their heads at this and laughed; but under his bright, bold eye their merriment died away, and the *marchef* said coldly: "Write him down Omar-bou-Skin."

He was in very deed without fear, if not quite without reproach. He proved it when he reddened with Musulman blood the sword the Roumis had entrusted to his hands. He was faithful in his treason, a deserter, yet a brave man. Every one must live. To live we must earn *douros*, and the Roumis have them to sell. God's ways are mysterious. They paid him by promotion, and bastard though he was, all held him to be of noble race.

Hidden in the rushes he waited patiently, having crept as close as he dared to the *haouch*. He had been prudent and had tried his ground yesterday; but he was still uncertain of success and anxious to know what was to come next. Presently the door opened, and he saw Afsia's white image appear on the threshold. He could not see the features, but only admire the delicacy of her shape and grace of movement. He thought she looked in the direction of the reeds, but just then Mansour appeared and she hastened away to her little garden.

"She has not said anything," Omar murmured to himself, as he saw the *Thaleb* seat himself calmly at the door.

He had foreseen from the first that she would keep her counsel, that without in the least knowing what evil was, she would feel a secret intuition this word "love" the goat had brought her so mysteriously yesterday had something to do with it, and like a true daughter of Fathma would wish to taste and try what it was.

There he remained motionless for long hours, studying the ground, like a chief of *goums* near a village he means to destroy. He watched all that went on about the *haouch*, the traffic to and fro, the dogs and above all the goat. The last came

up to crop the tufts of wild thyme close to the
reeds; he seized hold of her as he had done the
day before, and fastened to her horns a second "I
love you," which he had kept in readiness.

Like scouts who test the enemy's position by
throwing a random shot towards his advanced lines,
he made this second assault on Afsia's heart; then
creeping back to the high road, he once more
reached Djenarah at the hour of the midday siesta,
to find awaiting him in an alcove hung with Tu-
nisian *frechias*, eager-eyed and redolent of musk,
a brown-haired wanton of the *Ouled-Nayl*.

XXVI.

THE second message, like the first, found its ad-
dress; and like the first, it struck home. Night
and day Afsia thought of it.

A load of bliss seemed to weigh on her bosom.
She felt proud and happy. She was loved. Over-
whelmed by a wild intoxication of delight, she
thought her heart would burst, it beat so high.

Some one loved her, loved her! Her eyes were
moist and tears that were a pleasure rolled softly
down her cheeks. Twenty times a day she climbed
to her room, or took refuge in the thickest covert
of her oasis, to read and re-read, to turn and turn
again in her fingers, the two bits of cardboard
which the magic word "I love" made into talis-
mans of might.

She never wearied of repeating the word. It left her lips like a caress, a caress she would fain have followed each time by a kiss. She pronounced it to herself first, then half aloud, listening to her own lips forming the syllables and wondering at the effect it had upon her. " I love you! I love you! "—what a thrill of delight and mingled terror the words produced. And the rude song of the *tofla* of the *Beni-M'zab* her father had once dismissed his service, because she sang it before her, came back fresh and clear every word of it to her memory :

> I wait for my beloved!
> His look is proud and full of love.
> And when I hear his voice,
> Or the sound of his footfall,
> Or the neigh of his charger,
> I know them among a thousand ;
> And I feel like to die!

Ah! it was *her beloved* then who wrote the tender word, " I love you! " *Her Beloved !*—she had only a vague idea what it meant; and she was profoundly ignorant of men. Yet she felt she could love the unknown passionately. The unknown! unknown joy, unknown life, the sixth maiden sense, opening like a flower's cup to the hot sun of desire, something better than the bowl of fresh milk in thirsty weather, better than her bath under the poplars when the scorching *Simoom* blew.

Her Beloved!—what could it mean? She did

not know; she had been at no school where such
knowledge is imparted. She had never had a
little girl friend to breathe in her ear the poison
of bad thoughts; no man had ever touched her
heart, sullying it with bad wishes; no maid had
ever whispered her those words that startle young
girls, words they do not understand the first time,
but which make them blush the second time they
hear them. Virgin of soul, and body, and mind,
virgin of eyes and lips, as she was, yet all the
while she kept on murmuring to herself over and
over again:

"I wait for my Beloved!"

XXVII.

AGAIN next day she called the goat for the third
time, trembling with excitement. Her heart beat
wildly, and as the creature came slowly towards
her, stopping playfully at almost every step to crop
the shoots of the *diss*, she could see the little note
attached to one of its horns, and the sight filled
her with agitation and alarm. Suppose the *Thaleb*
were to discover it! She ran forward and in a
moment broke the silk thread and secured the prize,
concealing it in the usual hiding-place.

This time it was not merely a piece of cardboard
with the single word " Naabek;" but a folded paper,
a letter, a love-letter! What could be inside? She
was dying of impatience to know; but she waited

long before she dared read it, and at the spot where
the paper touched her breasts a red-hot iron seemed
to burn her. Two or three times she was on the
point of saying to Mansour:

"Look! *Thaleb*, what I found on Maaza's horns."
But Mansour would have said:

"Why did you not show it me before, child?"

And he would have weighed her with his search-
ing eye, his eye that saw everything, knew every-
thing,—except that for three days she had been guilty
of a wrong action.

"Yes! it must be wrong," she thought, "for I
dare not confess it. And now I am like the women
of Djenarah, I am hiding my thoughts; so perhaps
I am no longer a virgin."

Then after the evening meal when the *Thaleb*
had barred the door and had stretched himself across
it on his woollen carpet, and she had retired to the
safety of her own chamber and made sure he was
asleep, she lit her lamp and trembling all over drew
the letter from her bosom.

Pale with emotion she deciphered the burning
words, and as she drank in each sentence with
her eyes, a new feeling penetrated to her inmost
being.

"My tender gazelle," Omar had written, "your
gaze has wounded me like a scimitar. My heart
is bleeding with the stroke. I shall die, if you do
not heal me."

"Heal him? but how can I heal him?" Afsia

asked herself, and trembled.   But the remedy also
was made plain:

"If you do not wish me to die, to-morrow when
the sun shall touch the top of the *Djebel*, you must
turn towards the East and wave your *haïk*. I love
you!"

"Poor fellow!" thought Afsia. "What he asks
me is very easy to do! Well! well! is that all it
needs to heal him!"

XXVIII.

SHE slept little. All night long her imagination
drew in fair lines of blue on the golden background
of her dreams the likeness of the unknown lover,
wounded by her beauty to the death.

Where could he have seen her? But if he had
seen *her*, why! she might also have seen *him*. So
she searched her memory to recall the faces of all
the men her eyes had rested on during her last
journey to Djenarah; but she could remember none
that had interested her, only inquisitive or hostile
faces. There was nothing there to stir her heart,
nothing! Yet her eyes had done execution. A
man was yonder like to die. Like to die for having
seen her! Allah! Allah! she could not suffer that:
to-morrow she must, she would wave her *haïk*!

Old men too sleep little. Sleep is twin-brother
of death; it encroaches on life and filches many an
hour from it, and old men, the nearer they approach

the shadow of the tomb, the more eagerly save every moment they can from the night.

Next morning Mansour noticed how worn and weary her eyes looked after these hours of sleeplessness, and said:

"Why! what was there to disturb you so?"

"Nothing, my father," she replied, blushing scarlet at the idea he had discovered her secret thoughts, "only the mosquitoes made it impossible to sleep."

But the man of the world was suspicious, and retorted:

"Yes! the Tempter, Eblis the accursed, takes the form of a mosquito sometimes, to harass young folks and turn their heads. He keeps maids awake in the hours of darkness when the gates of evil are ajar, that they may peep within. O Afsia, flower of my life, apple of my eyes, home of my heart, beware your thoughts that linger on the accursed threshold do not overstep it."

Then, counting the days on his fingers:

"Three times twelve hours more, and the promised bride of El-Messaoud shall be his wife."

XXIX.

OMAR lay hid in the rushes awaiting the result of his manœuvres. He knew he had only to wait, and trust to destiny.

Stretched on his back he watched the sun descend slowly towards the *Djebel*, reddening the West with

its glowing colours. Far away on the plain great
brown camels were cropping the white bunches of
alpha-grass and the green tufts of *diss* that pierced
here and there through the rocky soil; a group of
little camel-boys, tattered and half-naked, were sitting
in a circle with all the calm *aplomb* of old men,
and seemed to be discussing the topics of the day,
while far off on the horizon wrapped in a cloud of
topaz-blue mist the minaret of the *ksour* gleamed
white in vivid contrast to the dark blue of the hills
lit up by the last glow of the setting sun.

When the fiery disc appeared to touch the
mountain-top, Omar turned and looked towards the
haouch. He saw the master standing at the door,
apparently scanning every corner of the marsh with
his scrutinizing gaze.

" Can the girl have been a little fool," he thought,
" and betrayed my secret ? "

But in another instant she appeared, and he saw
her direct her steps towards the garden.

She took up a position where Mansour could not
see her, and slowly undoing her *haïk*, she waved
it three times towards the West.

" She is mine ! " said Omar to himself, and laughed.
And without waiting longer he set off to return
to the town.

XXX.

So confident was he of success that he now let two
days slip quietly by without a further . attempt.

Artful schemer, he meant the girl to grow impatient, for impatience is the mother of hasty decisions and rash deeds.

Besides he required time for deliberation, to think out the best way to secure his object. The consent of the lady is always a great point gained, in fact the main point, but it is not everything. Material obstacles may thwart your wishes and unforeseen eventualities upset your calculations. Chance often spoils " the best laid schemes," and has got to be reckoned with.

His host too kept saying, " No hurry! no hurry! watch and wait."

So he waited till the very day before the wedding.

He had counted on Afsia's innocence, and the result had justified his expectations.

After waving her *haïk*, she fled in confusion, as if she had been committing a crime, then ran to find her goat and was bitterly disappointed at there being no fresh letter for her.

What had happened seemed so extraordinary to her, and her ideas had been so utterly upset by this sudden and violent change in her tranquil life that she felt nothing was impossible,—except that the ordinary course of events should continue.

She hoped and feared, expecting with beating heart and strained nerves some grand event to happen in the night. She woke up several times with a start, trembling like a leaf stirred by the wind at the least growl of the dogs.

"There he is," she whispered, "there he is per-
haps. What will he do?"

Two days passed by. She never thought of her
approaching marriage; she forgot completely she
was to change her whole life next day, and her
eyes remained fixed on the reeds of the marsh of
Ain-Chabrou, from which she expected every mo-
ment to see the unknown spring up.

The third day her patience gave out. Curiosity,
the consuming wish to know the truth, vanquished
prudence altogether; she made a pretence of search-
ing for the flowers of the *chicch*, and all the time
playing with her goat, drew nearer and nearer to the
tufts of reeds.

XXXI.

SHE was half singing, half humming, as she went,
the song of the *Beled-el-Djerid*, the song she had
heard but once when she was quite a child, but
which she remembered so well.

"Oh, ho!" said Omar to himself, who watched
her from his post of observation, "the gazelle is not
so shy to-day. Like ourselves, the daughters of
Fathma are children of sin. Keep watch and ward
on them, careful guardians and jealous duennas,
lavish precautions, advice, and bolts and bars to
secure them; it is all in vain! They will still burn
with eagerness to lose the treasure you take such
pains to guard. They love vice before they know

what vice is. Nature is stronger than morality, and
what we call virtue is a mere matter of opportunity,
—or its absence, and individual temperament. Here
is a maid the women of Djenarah vaunt as worthy
to add her name to the list of the four the Prophet
counted perfect women, and lo! she comes running
to meet an unknown lover, inquisitive and wanton
as a heifer in heat."

Hidden in the high tufts of the iris, he watched
her coming slowly nearer and nearer, without how-
ever being seen by her; and her beauty positively
dazzled him.

"She is lovelier than I thought," he murmured;
"she is worth all the douros of the *khasnadji*. If
only the old goat could have for just one quarter
of an hour a good ophthalmia to burn his eyes
blind, or a sudden palsy to nail him to his mat;—
or better still a sound whack over the skull that
would keep him stunned whilst I make his kid my
own, and let him come to again as soon as I cry:
'Done! old man; the deed is done!'"

She glided along beside the irises, brushing the
flowers with her *gandourah*, and when she was only
a few steps from him, he called in a low voice:

"*Tofla! tofla!* I am here. I love you! Come
this way. Lie down among the rushes, the old man
has not seen you!"

She trembled at the sound of his voice. The
Spahi had done his best to speak gently, but his
tone frightened the girl as if it had been a threat.

Her heart beat violently, and she was ready to faint.

She dared not turn her head, and walked on. She would have run, but her limbs bent under her.

At this moment she heard the *Thaleb* calling. "Afsia! Afsia!"

The familiar voice she loved did her good. She turned in its direction, and started to return to the *haouch* with rapid steps.

"Why do you wander so far away?" he asked. "I like not your going near the marsh! Have I not told you before that Satan the Poisoner lurks under its dark tangles? His mouth breathes fever,—and whispers bad words into maidens' ears."

Afsia made no reply. She avoided going near the *Thaleb*, dreading to betray the agitation that paled her cheeks; and going to the back of the house she sat down beside the brook.

There she began to think,—of the voice that had terrified her so, of the lover who was lying hid yonder. How silly she had been, and how cowardly. It was *he*, her lover; he loved her, and would not have hurt her. Why had she not lain down in the rushes, as he had begged her. The *Thaleb* would not have seen her then, and she would have beheld *him*, could have consoled him and told him not to die. And instead of that, she had never answered, and had run away like a mad girl! Oh! how stupid and rude and awkward he must think her! It is all over, he would never love her any more!

And sore at heart with vexation, she began to pull great handfuls of flowers and toss them into the stream.

"Eh! Afsia, why drown the poor flowers you love so well?"

XXXII.

He had approached her without her hearing his footfall, and was now looking down on her with a smile.

"You are angry," he went on, "you frown."

"Yes!" she answered with the pettish tone of a spoilt child; "I cannot walk a step before me, I cannot turn to right or left, without hearing your voice calling after me, and saying: Where are you going?"

"You must forgive me," said the *Thaleb* gently, sitting down by her side; "you are my fortune, and I go in constant fear of losing you, for if I lost you, I should have lost my life. By the all-merciful God, I will not have you expose yourself to the risk of having the treasure you possess stolen, the treasure I have guarded for fourteen years with so much pains."

"What treasure?"

"A jewel as precious as the most precious diamond in the Sultan of Stamboul's diadem; a pearl the like of which the Prince of the Faithful has not and has never had in his seraglio!"

"I possess no treasure," exclaimed Afsia, looking at the *Thaleb* with amazement. "I have no jewels but my silver ear-rings, my silver anklets and brace- lets, and this little finger-ring you told me was given you by the first woman you loved; and all these belong to you, for it was you gave them me."

"And have you nothing else?"

"Yes! myself, my whole body; I belong to you, I am your daughter and your slave. To-morrow I shall be your wife,—but still your true slave, and daughter."

"My own Afsia, my rose of sweetness!" cried Mansour, who felt himself purified and rejuvenated, in presence of such youth and innocence, "you are like the *houris* the Prophet bestows on the faithful who, made light by their good deeds, have been able to cross the sharp-edged *Sirak*, and now float amid the delights of the gardens of the Elect."

"Have *houris* then a treasure to give as well?"

"Even as you have, my love, my life! The Prophet forgive me, if I blaspheme, but theirs is not so precious as yours."

She remained in deep thought, while Mansour gazed at her in silence, filled with love and pride.

He, the man of pleasure, so long given up to sin, seducer, adulterer, he had wrought this price- less work of art, this jewel of the world, this pearl among pearls, this flower of flowers. She was of marriageable age and still chaste, a virgin of un- sullied purity of mind, a maid immaculate as the snow that covers in cold winters the high crests of the *Djurjura*, as the bud of the palm that half unfolds on a morning of springtide to the first kiss of the sun.

He gazed at her tenderly, enjoying the wonder that sparkled in her great liquid eyes.

XXXIII.

"To-morrow is the great day, dear Afsia; you must bid farewell to our *haouch*, to the little fountain and the poplar you used to bathe under; farewell to your garden where you loved to hide yourself for hours together, to the birds that used to greet your awakening, to the reeds of the marsh that stripe the grey plain with their line of green, to the distant blue hill where the sun sets, to the desert, the sands and the *Simoom*."

"I am sad," said Afsia.

"Sad! but why? Yonder will be neither sand nor *Simoom;* you will have a garden as fair as this one, and the birds will sing at your awakening as sweetly as they do here. Your new house is finer than the Caïd's own, its floors are of enamelled tile-work, and there is a court where great orange trees bloom; there is a fountain-jet and gold fish that swim in the bason."

"I am sad," said Afsia.

"Listen what you shall have more: a cool, shady gallery, its gratings of woodwork painted red, and wreathed in vine and honeysuckle and the many-coloured bells of the graceful bindweed.

" There you will take your siesta, and the curtain of foliage will be so thick you will but just catch a glimpse of the blue of the sky. Under your feet you shall have carpets of Tunis; you shall have bright shawls of silk to wrap around you, a vest braided with gold such as the women of Constantine wear, and red slippers of gold and blue-silk embroidery."

" I am sad," said Afsia, " sad, sad."

" Throw off your sadness, dear child; it clouds my soul. Why grow sad at the very hour when so many maids are overjoyed? What will the women say, when they come to lead you to the wedding to-morrow, if they see you anxious-eyed? They will think the old harridans with the evil eye have cast a spell over your betrothals, and that you weep because you hate your intended husband."

" Then they would think wrong! for I love you well. It is not that makes me sad...."

Afsia hesitated, and was on the point of revealing her secret; but he continued, fearing to hear the naïve child avow it was his grey beard that saddened her on the eve of her marriage-day:

" Clear the clouds from your face, moon of my soul; henceforth your kindly light must be the lantern of my nights. Oh! how shall I repay you for all the happiness you will give me. I would be the fringe of your *haïk*, to be with you all the day long; or better still, I would be a ringlet of your dark hair, to be with you night and day. I would be the *Meroued* that darkens your eyes, or better the colour of ripe pomegranate that reddens your lips. Up! up! beloved of my heart, dry your eyes, your fountain has tears enough. Away! and put on your brave attire."

" Where shall you be, Mansour, when the women come for me?"

" I shall follow your mule on a thorough-bred the Caïd will send me, a horse descended from a certain black stallion, that was son of a mare of my father's, on whose back I won renown; and I shall watch with drawn sword over the treasure God has given me!"

XXXIV.

SHE retired to put on her finest braveries, those Mansour had bought her on his last visit to the town.

She braided her heavy ebon locks, thick as the *berima* the noble sons of the tents wind round their heads, and which fell in lovely silken threads on either side of her shoulders the sun had so often kissed, put on a *gandourah* of so fine a texture the rosy tints of her flesh were visible through the woof, and enveloped her hips in the ample drawers of yellow silk, leaving her calves bare. Then she drew tightly round her loins the many-hued *foutah*, clasped her broad golden girdle, and taking a hand-mirror seated herself among her woollen cushions, and chewing the while the branch of *souak* that scents the breath and makes the lips red, fell to admiring herself in the mirror.

Like a child its mother has dressed out in new clothes, not daring to move for fear of soiling its finery and disarranging the symmetrically ordered folds, she sat there motionless, triumphant, smiling at her own loveliness.

She no longer thought of her coming marriage, nor of Mansour, nor yet of the man lurking in the rushes, nor of the messages he had written her, nor of his voice that had frightened her so; she thought of nothing but the fair sight she saw in her mirror,—and of a surety she could hardly have seen a fairer.

And to add a further brilliancy to her charms and the glory of her radiant, smiling beauty, the father of the world that had aided the blossoming of the wonder, reddened her lips and dyed her rosy cheeks, filled out her bosom and lit up her eyes,—the sun, the glorious sun, came back a moment from his setting to pay her homage.

A sunbeam shot suddenly through the trellis of her window, bathing in its rays, as though for a last caress before it departed for ever, the virginity that had budded and ripened under its kisses. As one hangs round a beloved friend, whom one is to see no more, unable to tear oneself away, em-

bracing him, then pushing him back, then turning
to embrace him once more, and saying " Good-
bye! good-bye!"—the fond beam enwrapped her,
shining on her face, playing in the blue depths of
her hair, flashing on her silver ear-rings, her brace-
lets and anklets, glittering on the row of sequins
that framed her brown cheeks and the gold spangles
of her cap of purple velvet, quivering over her
body, penetrating everywhere, throwing in every
direction sudden gleams and sudden eclipses of
light, torrents of yellow shadows, floods of red
radiance, cascades of fire, scattering at every move-
ment of her figure dancing effects of light and
shade.

·The centre of all this scintillating brilliance, the
child looked like one of those female idols you see
blazing with artificial lights, before which in the
mysterious recesses of some chapel, the idolatrous
worshippers of Jesus bow down. Like these eternal
symbols of human degradation, she was surrounded
with perfumes intoxicating and disturbing to the
strongest heads. From a tiny copper chafing-dish
that stood in front of her, rose the blue fumes of
fragrant pastilles, while from the folds of her clothing
and hollow of her bosom breathed the concentrated
scent of roses. The subtle, delicious poison filled
the *oda* (upper chamber), diffusing an atmosphere of
indolence and languor. Beware of these enervating
perfumes. In your Churches they bend women's souls
to the priestly yoke; in our land amid the luxurious

cushions of the alcove and behind the curtain of the women's tent, brave men and strong are bent to the will of puny woman.   They deliver up to the weakest slip of a girl hard, rugged soldiers, bound hand and foot and humble as the negro slaves our caravans brought in former days from the sun-scorched lands beyond the desert to sell to the Christian traders.   Wherefore, if you would remain a man, tarry not in the company of women.

He that lives in their midst, grows at heart a eunuch.   As surely as the knife strips the eunuch of his carnal, generative parts, the influences that radiate from woman rob the man who is ever in her society of all manliness of soul.

This is written, or words to this effect, in the sayings of the wise Lockman, who is none other than Solomon the Great.

When the *Thaleb* softly pushed open the door of the *oda*, he fell into an ecstasy, ravished by what he saw, feeling the fire of thirty course again through his veins, and his heart grow tender.

And before this unequalled nosegay of loveliness, rose and violet, hyacínth and lily, blooming there amid the heady odours of incense, before this beautiful idol, decked out with gay attire and lighted up for worship by the last fires of the setting sun, he stretched forth his hands in adoration and fell upon his knees.

XXXV.

THE sun disappeared behind the mountains, shooting a last ray to kiss the face of the *tofla*, lighting up once more the sparkles of her sequins and her ornaments, so that she seemed to Mansour's dazzled eyes a goddess of flesh and blood, filling the *oda* with emanations of light and fragrance.

Then twilight absorbed the scene, leaving the glitter of their eyes as the only luminous points.

They gazed into each other's eyes, he panting, agitated, excited, she wondering, but calm and grave. At sight of the old man on his knees before her, no smile of mockery stirred her lips. She thought simply these were the usual preliminaries a husband must perform, and was on the point of asking what *she* should do.

But her courage failed her, for fear he should smile at her ignorance. Then as he still remained kneeling, devouring her with his eyes, she took his head between her hands and kissed him on the forehead.

He trembled at the touch of her lips, and passed his burning hands down the curves of her girlish shape.

"Light of my life, why do you kiss me?"

"Because I love you."

"How do you love me," said the old man, deliciously stirred and flattered by her caress,—"as a father or as a lover?"

"I do not know. I love you because you are good and kind; because you have watched over my childhood, because you give me all I wish. But I am ready to love you in any way you wish. Only tell me how you wish it to be, and as I am to be your wife, teach me how a wife should love."

And proud of her answer, she waited to hear his approval.

"O lake of purity!" murmured Mansour, "who should dare to sully your crystal soul!"

And pressing a long kiss on her little hands with their rose-pink nails, he rose from his knees, dreading to lose the mastery over his feelings. He was afraid he might be tempted to rob himself! So, his brain fired by love and confused by the heady scents, his energy of purpose tottering, he hurried from the chamber, descended the stairs and crossing the room below, opened the door of the *haouch.*

Standing on the threshold, he gazed at the Western sky still glowing with the rays of the departing sun like a huge fiery furnace into which the Almighty had tossed all the kingdoms of the earth, and he seemed to watch his own happiness melt in the mighty conflagration.

"In the name of the God of Mercy," he cried, "let no wind of disaster arise this night, let no storm arise to trouble the serenity of to-morrow!"

XXXVI.

At this moment the dogs barked, and a child's voice cried in long-drawn monotous tones:

"Thaleb! Ho! Thaleb-El-Mansour! Ho! Sidi-Thaleb!"

"What is it?" the *Thaleb* asked sharply.

And he perceived a little boy of some ten years old standing still, two hundred yards away in the direction of the marsh, holding a dog in leash.

"Can I come near?" said the child, "will your *slouguis* not hurt me?"

"They are chained; what is your business with me?"

"Why!" said the boy, coming forward some paces, "I come from the Sheikh Ben-Kaouiadi, Sheik of the village yonder at the far end of the plain; he sends you his bitch to serve your *slouguis*."

"The foul fiend take you and your bitch and your Sheikh!" cried Mansour; "off with you, my fine fellow!"

"The beast has a right good pedigree," retorted the child, quite unmoved, "and Sidi-ben-Kaouiadi would like her to have a litter by your dogs."

"Go tell him if he wants dogs, he must make them himself; now be off, or I will loose mine at your backside!"

The *slouguis*, who scented the female, began to growl with eagerness to be free.

The boy hesitated a while as though not knowing

what to do; at last he made up his mind, and started slowly homewards, dragging the bitch after him, that followed reluctantly, stopping at every corner of the road.

"I'll go myself," muttered Mansour angrily, " and rate the fool, this insolent Sheikh, sending his bitch to me to couple with my dogs. A pretty picture for Afsia, on the eve of her wedding-day!"

And he followed the little *Bedouin* with his eyes, as he plunged deeper and deeper among the rushes of the marsh, a point of grey vanishing in the blackness.

The splendours of the setting sun had faded little by little, and nothing was left but a faint red glow, while the evening star climbed the sky.

XXXVII.

PRESENTLY those mysterious sounds that are never heard in the daytime rose in the sombre dark. Jackals, hyænas, wild cats, horned vipers, black scorpions, little grey serpents with emerald eyes, crept about the ways, seeking their food. All the rabble rout of night-prowlers, haunters of waste places, gaunt hungry marauders,—slimy reptiles, night birds and beasts of prey,—the grim host of plunderers that sally forth when good men lie down to sleep, and raven to fill their belly when others are full, began to rustle in the gloom.

Why has God made creatures that must be gaunt

and famished? why has he not given abundance
to all?   This is what the vulgar herd say, forgetting
that every good thing must be won by effort.   So,
for such as do not get their share, the Master has
given the night,—the harvest time of the weak
and poor.   You refuse him sustenance,—well then,
he will rob you to get it.

It is for you, glutted with plenty as you are, to
guard your store.

As night fell, gloom descended on Mansour's
spirit.

In the morning all had seemed bright and gay,
the whole world full of joy and content; now his
soul was so mournful it might have been following
his own body to the grave, borne on the funeral
bier and wrapped in the green shroud.

"And yet," he said, listening to the distant cries
that pierced the dark like warning voices, "*why*
should these sounds make me sad?   The night-
robbers have no grudge against you or yours; you
have nought to fear.   You know them well.   Have
you not brushed past them a hundred times travelling
by night, in those days when you too prowled the
dark like them to glut your appetite?   You met
them many a time at the turn of a path or at the
edge of the *bush*, and you said, 'Pass on.'
Then each went his way, where hunger drove us.

"Ah! those were good times, good times indeed,
when I robbed my pittance from those more for-
tunate than myself who had an over-abundance of

the world's goods. And why did they not guard
their womankind better, these gluttons, wallowing
insolently in every luxury? My game was to prey
on others' goods, and I won it, for women love
the bold. Now it is my turn to watch and ward
my own.

"Chaouias, Hadars, Giaours, I defied and braved
you all, when I was young; I am old now, but I
still brave you and defy you. So long as I was
strong, you called me the *Happy Man*, because I
knew how to carve my way to success; but since
my beard had grown grey, you have known me
as the Madman. You have mocked me, you have
shouted with laughter, you and your wives with
you, saying: 'How painfully he keeps guard over
his treasure; a thief will have it for all that.' Well!
let him come now, this thief; for the hour is close
at hand when no thief can rob me of my darling
any more!"

So saying, he lifted up his manly voice and cried
a warning cry, that rang out over the desert where
all else but he were wrapped in silence and asleep.

"Beware! beware! if any thief is prowling round
this house, he is prowling to meet his death."

XXXVIII.

AFSIA slipped trembling to his side, and her gentle
voice recalled him to himself, whispering softly:
"Who is it you threaten so fiercely?"

He smiled without answering her question.

" I hear nothing," she went on, after a moment's silence, " nothing but the yelping of the jackals and the noise of horses' feet yonder towards Alloufa. Why are you here at the door? come indoors."

He took her by the waist, and pushed her gently within the house.

All preparations for departure were complete. The articles they were to take away with them lay ready for removal—clothes, bright-hued *frechias*, the beautiful Koran illuminated and written from end to end by the hand of the *Thaleb* El-Hadj-Ali-bou-Nahr, the most skilled copyist and illuminator in all the province of Constantine,—and your humble servant, Mansour's *flissas* with hafts of carved wood and scabbards of red leather, his long gun with barrel of damascined steel and silver rings, the gun that had made so many women widows and mothers childless, and his bridle with eylet-holes finished in gold and silken thread, worn and slashed in countless fights, bridle of the beautiful mare,—foal of the son of Naama, that he had ridden on days of battle, and his ringing stirrups and his silver spurs arabesqued in rude patterns,— old servants preserved through all perils and vicissitudes! What memories each article recalled! what struggles! what crises of love and war! how many hours, light or heavy, gay with laughter or murderous with hate! Now all this past, mournful and radiant at once, he piled pellmell in one huge *fondouk*.

Then when the oaken coffer was shut to, when he had cast round him a last look, had once again inspected Afsia's chamber, he pushed the chest against the door of the stairway and sat down on it, resting as it were on the ashes of his past life, henceforth turning his gaze only to the future.

The future! It lay before him radiant with happiness to come; it had dark eyes like stars, all shining with promises of bliss, and they looked at him and smiled. ...

He beckoned, and the bride of to-morrow drew near, and leant her weight on his sturdy breast,— a load of delight, a burden of joy, a mass of happiness; something soft and sweet like a pet bird that rustles its wings between a woman's breasts, like quivering lips kissing a girl's body that is faint with desire.

Sweet, tender form! He longed to hold it safe in his very heart, caged and hidden there, a prisoner till the morrow.

XXXIX.

AFSIA had heard the boy's voice plainly, and it had filled her with apprehension. She felt now that she had done wrong to keep silence about her adventure, for some instinct told her mischief was plotting in the dark,—and that through her own fault. She burned to make a clean breast, but did not know how to tell the tale of all that had happened, and above all how to begin her confession. She opened her mouth to reveal the secret, but blushes covered her cheeks and her tongue seemed frozen. So she pressed closer to Mansour, mentally asking pardon from the bottom of her heart for the fault she had been guilty of against him.

On his side, he looked into her eyes, drawing her to him with feverish hands. Apparently calm and indifferent, he was in truth as deeply stirred as a boy at his first assignation. He had to go back in memory to the far-off days of his lawless passion for his father's bride, Meryem, to recall so fierce an emotion. Ah! the long, weary hours he had lived through since! How many weeks, and months, and years had passed since then! The white threads in his beard had long ago overmastered the black; yet he felt the furious passions of twenty rise within him and howl to be satisfied!

He looked, and saw her arms resting on the rounded hips, and her virgin bosom rising and falling softly as she breathed.

He saw his darling white and fair, a creature of grace and beauty, in all the seductive charm of her brave attire and scented raiment!

So she was his, this fair girl, his only, all his! She was his very own, his chattel, his bride, his wife; he could taste his joy now, on the instant, if he so wished. The thought made his blood as fire; while the burning *Simoom* that had been blowing

all day, the toilette the girl had made, the odours
that breathed from her, her innocent caresses that
stirred his blood, the warm evening breeze entering
by the half-open door, the hot night air laden with
amorous influences, the nightingale singing in the
poplars, and further away the low mournful cries
that rose amid the reeds greeting the peaceful
moonrise,—all called to him, "Take her! take her
now! she is yours."

XL.

NOT far off a lamp of red earthenware stood on a
stool, and threw a mysterious reddish glow over the
oda, while in one corner lay unrolled a large mat
of *diss* fibre with thick woollen cushions arranged
on it. Here they were to rest till the wedding-
guests should arrive at the first peep of dawn to
conduct the pair to the town.

Mansour pointed to it, pushing her from him
almost roughly.

"Go and sleep, dear child!"

Dear *child!* Yes! Yesterday she was still a
child; but to-day she seemed to him a woman, he
knew not why. Hitherto his heart had loved her,
now his senses longed for her. A few hours had
wrought the change; he pushed her from him,
afraid of his own weakness.

She withdrew obediently; and Mansour unfastening
his rosary from his neck, began to pass the ivory

beads one by one through his fingers, saying half aloud for each, as if to drown the thoughts that *would* assail him, the sacred name of Allah.

For it is written in the Book how this Name drives away unholy desires.

Meantime Afsia had sat down as he bade her on her cushions; but as he repeated for the hundredth time the name of God, she thought she heard a cry of distress break out clear and distinct amid the yelping of the jackals.

She rose instantly and ran to take refuge at the *Thaleb's* feet.

"Do you hear it?" she cried; "oh! I am frightened."

And pressing close to his breast once more, she hid her face under his *burnouse*.

He took the child's head between his hands, and fell to kissing her thick dark locks.

She did not resist, happy to feel safe. It was a father fondling her; she thought of him in no other light. Had the moment come to confess the secret that had been tormenting her for days? But suddenly he straightened himself and pushed her away again. Then he ran to the door, and scrutinized the outer darkness.

Some one was in distress yonder. He hardly gave it a thought; he was counting the hours to wait before the wedding-guests should arrive, and saying:

"If only they could come sooner!"

"I am frightened," repeated Afsia once again,

following him and clinging to his arm, " I am fright-
ened! Don't go. Listen, Mansour, I have something
to tell you. Stay with me. Don't leave me! Don't
leave me!"

XLI.

STAY with her! this was exactly what 'he feared
to do, for he had just been caught by that fury of
desire that seizes men,— and they say women too
sometimes,—on the eve of passing the threshold of
old age. This is the critical time of love, as it is
of life. Passion takes fire, and explodes like a
weapon loaded by an awkward hand. Men who
have overpassed maturity, and play the game of
young lovers, hurt themselves and are hooted by
others.

He by no means wished to be hooted. He loved
the girl, but he did not love to be laughed at, and
he would certainly be the laughing-stock of Djenarah
to-morrow, if by any chance he should give way
to his longings.

And yet again and again in the course of a very
few minutes the instant had come when he could
barely be called master of himself, when he was
on the point of plundering himself by deflowering
his own bride on the eve of the wedding-day, and
making himself the butt of never-ending mockery
for the rest of his life. For think of the scandal when
the matron, throwing open the window at the peep of

day, should present to the impatient crowd a sheet without a stain, to be greeted with shouts of laughter!

" By the Prophet! " they would cry, "for fourteen years the old ass has kept watch and ward over the bride he took right from the mother's womb to be quite certain of her maidenhood,—and the wedding-night she has not left a spot on her bed! God's curse is surely upon him! Is he so weakly and exhausted, this old seducer of women? or has the bird he kept encaged, slipt through the bars under his very nose? Tahan! Tahan! cuckold! cuckold! "

Why! yes, they would shout this and many another insult at him, and point the finger of scorn at his shame-faced figure slipping shyly along under the houses, his hood drawn over his eyes like a pauper, and his *burnouse* wrapped tight round his tall thin form.

He would choose the lonely streets, seek out the shade, lurk under walls; but some passer-by would always discover him, and nudge his companion and point at him; or it would be some *enfant terrible* of the streets, who would shout at the top of his voice:

" Ho! *Thaleb!* Ho! ho! cuckold! Who was your wife's lover before you? "

Or perhaps it would be an old woman, one of his former light-o'-loves, that would spit on his hood, showing her yellow teeth.

XLII.

HE had taken his stick and was striding up and
down before the door, beating the air with it as if
he were striking the heads of his mockers, seeming
to hear already their hooting and laughter.

"No! that shall never be; the ruffians shall never
have cause to cast insult at me: Hadars and
Chaouias, you know what I am called.

"I am called Happy, the Happy Man, and to the
hour of my death, you shall continue to kiss my
stirrup and salute me Lord!

"No! I say no! Though the maid should fall on
her knees to me, should put her lips on mine,
winding her arms round me like an ivy-branch, my
heart and my senses shall be cold as the marble of
the mosque."

And the maid did actually call him, standing at
the threshold and begging him:

"Mansour, Mansour! come back to me."

"Go in, my gazelle," returned the *Thaleb*. "I
do not wish you to follow me. Unfasten the dogs,
and let them stay by you on guard! Hear you
yonder cries of distress? I must run as far as the
first rushes bordering the marsh."

"Mansour, don't go there, I beseech you. Satan
the Foul Fiend is hid in the reeds, spreading his
sorcerer's net like a great spider."

The *Thaleb* smiled at her words—words she had
learned from him.

" Fear not, dear child! He spreads his nets only
for girls, for women and weaklings; men like my-
self break the web with one blow of their stick.
There is nothing to fear yonder, nothing but a
silly boy who came here just now, and who has
no doubt slipped into some boghole. I recognize
his voice. The curse of heaven would light on me,
if I left the child to drown."

" Leave me not alone, Mansour, I swear there is
some evil design afloat. Come back; listen, I have
a confession on my lips."

But Mansour, fearing a fresh assault on his pas-
sions, only cried:

" What! a confession, my gazelle of innocence!
You shall make it when I come back. There is
nothing to fear; the dogs are good watch-dogs, and
I shall be within sight of the *haouch* all the time.
Stay within-doors, *tofla*, and shoot the bolts."

And he started to run.

XLIII.

HE ran on lost in thought, and without heeding
the way he came, reached the spot where the soil
is moist and the iris begins to grow thick on the
marshy soil.

Then stopping, he heard the voice in front of him
crying lamentably, " Help! help! "

" Ho! you, where are you, wretched boy? " the
Thaleb shouted back. " You undertook to run the

devil's errands, and the devil has left you in
the lurch on the road. You are stuck in the mud,
and your villainy with you! and there you may
stop!"

"Save me, save me!" sobbed the child.

Mansour was pushing his way further into the
rushes, following the path that winds in and out
round the stagnant pools when he suddenly noticed
his dogs were following him.

Startled at sight of the bludgeon their master
was brandishing in the air to scare invisible enemies,
they advanced noiselessly, questing for a scent, but
keeping at a respectful distance from the *Thaleb.*

He could see their eyes glittering amid the black
rushes.

"Infernal beasts," he shouted savagely at them,
"what do you mean by following me? Who bade
you come, mongrel hounds? Why do you track
my steps like ill-omened *djinns*, you wretches? go
home, you villains! go home, you thieves!"

And he hurled his stick at them.

The dogs scurried away at full speed, ears down
and tails between their legs; but presently all three
stopped, watching their master's disappearing form.

The latter had started running again, for the
pitiful voice sounded louder than ever, with its
despairing cry for "help, help!" but always at the
same distance and from the farther side of one of
the channels through the swamp. To get there, he
must make a detour.

He stopped, hesitating about going so far away, and cast a look behind.

The *haouch* was already a long way off. He might still have distinguished its white outline, if the night had been clear; but a heavy cloud was across the moon and he could see nothing of it. He could not even make out the trees of the oasis that sheltered the house in an arbour of refreshing greenery. All was hidden under the heavy, brooding shadows.

XLIV.

BUT the boy's voice continued to call for help, each moment more pitiful, and he went on.

He had already passed the sombre line of rushes, and stood on the brink of the marsh itself, that stretched before him a great black sheet of water, dotted here and there by the sharp points of tall reeds.

He listened; but the cries had ceased. Nothing to be heard but the distant barking of the jackals on the plain, and near at hand the flapping wings of some waterfowl startled from sleep and the splashing of the frogs diving into the deep black water.

In his turn, he shouted; but the only answer was the light rustle of the wind in the grass. Out on the swamp there were strange grumblings and mutterings, while weird gleams of light flashed amid dense patches of shadow. Then suddenly the pools of water would stand out of a dull, dead white.

He shouted again:

"Where are you? devil's brat, where are you?"

But there was no reply, and Mansour, who had never known what fear was, felt a shudder that nipped the heart.

"It is the hellish hour," he thought, "when the *djinns* are abroad," and said to himself what he had shouted just before to his dogs: "Home! go home!"

At the same moment he heard a loud noise in the tall grass not far from him. And going forward he saw the black figures of the *slouguis*, one of them coupling with the bitch, while the other two fought savagely, growling and rolling over and over each other in the mire of the swamp.

XLV.

YES! the *haouch* was plunged in darkness and disaster. Too long it had gladdened the plain with its red-tiled roof and white walls and the fair green oasis around it. Too long it had echoed to the merry laugh of its mistress and the gay songs of her birds. Its day of brightness is over; and gloomy clouds lower in the sky. Hitherto sorrow had passed by forgetful, but now stays its flight, and shakes over the peaceful roof its tear-laden wing.

Each in turn; and it is sorrow's turn now,— sorrow that is twin-brother of death, and anticipates death in exacting the poll-tax of tears our lives are condemned to pay. All pass through its rude hands, for scarce any of the righteous have had wisdom to escape them.

" To-day for me, to-morrow for thee " is the motto inscribed over the portal of the graveyard, the menace they that still laugh or weep are confronted with, when they see the dead man given to the worms. But above all it is the phrase the happy must needs hear in the midst of their festivities from the lips of the unfortunate.

Young man, smiling at life with wanton eyes, tasting the rosy sweets of your mistress' bosom, resting your head on the soft pillow of her breasts, haste, haste to take your fill of laughter and of love, for misfortune stands there at your side watching and waiting her hour to chill for ever warm lips and loving heart alike.

" Allah! Allah! why such pain?" groans the poor creature, surprised by the dismal visitant.

But he replies in this wise:

" Fool! search your own heart, and you will see only yourself to blame for the hostility of fate. Look into your past. Have you not worn a wide enough road? Twenty years you have been at work levelling a way for me. I passed by, and saw it,— a broad straight highway; I took it, and lo! I am here."

And behold one that knocks at the door of the *haouch*, and says:

" It is I; lo! I am here."

"You! you?" cried the girl, whiter than her white *haïk*.

"Yes! I; you expected me."

"I expected no one. Who are you?"

"I! you know who I am,—your lover, the man that loves you, who is dying of love! Open, open to me!"

"You!" murmured the trembling Afsia, "you who wrote me you would die. I dare not open the door; I ought not to, and oh! I am frightened."

"Maiden, your face is more radiant than the morning-star; your voice is more melodious than the instruments of music at a feast. Maiden more delightful to the eyes than the date-trees of the oasis, fresher than the fountain that leaps from the living rock, tell me what it is you fear, you who can impose your will on men as absolutely as a Sultana on the negroes of the seraglio."

"Begone! begone!" cried Afsia.

"Oh! let me come in; you are my fountain, and I am athirst. I am a palm parched for the waters of the well, that dies for lack of moisture. Open to me; my throat is dry with love."

During all the long hours he had lain in the tall rushes of the marsh, he had had ample leisure to compose these fine speeches, golden nets that catch weak women's hearts.

"I cannot open to you," replied Afsia. "The *Thaleb* El-Mansour, my master, forbade me. And I must not speak to any other man, for he makes me his wife to-morrow, Leave me, sir stranger; to-morrow from earliest dawn I shall be at Djenarah, and if you would look on me, join the wedding-guests. There will be room at the feast for all."

"What! it is true then! this old man, with one foot already in the grave, is to put the other in your bed? He has deceived himself; it is not you, it is death should be his bride. True they told me it was to be so, but I could not credit them. I said, 'Your words are dictated by spite, and they are not true. No! no! the rose of Djenarah can never wed this ruin of a man.' But now I *must* believe it, for you confess yourself it is true. To think of such a fate hanging over your head by just a thread! Have you reflected well? he takes advantage of your simplicity and innocence! Yet you have eyes, you can see. Or has he cast a spell over you, bald-headed vulture of the sinister eye, that you agree to put your youth and beauty and unsullied maidenhood in his cold, age-stiffened arms? He can give you no pleasure, with him you will know nothing of love's ecstasy. But tender bud, he will pluck you rudely from the stalk before ever you have felt your petals unfold; you will fade away beneath the icy breath; you will wither up on the arid soil. To your last hour you will weep your maidenhood, your happiness and youth, blighted and destroyed, Think! think what you do! You crave the love of the young, you whose eyes are stars and your mouth a fountain of delight. Open

to me, and I will give you a foretaste of the joys
of Paradise."

"I cannot. Do not speak to me so. I will hear
no more such words. Begone!"

"What! did you bid me come, only to drive me
away again? Did you not wave your *haïk*, as I
asked you? did I *force* you to give the signal we
agreed on?"

"I knew not what you meant, when you asked
me to do it. But I see now I have done wrong.
You sent me sweet words, and I was fain to see
his face who sent them."

"Well then! I am here. Open the door, and
you shall see my face."

"I do not wish to see it, for I have done wrong,
and I have felt remorse, and I should be doing
wrong again if I saw it. Leave me; Mansour
will soon return, and if he found you at the door...."

"Have no fear. The old man is far enough. He
has to do with a very cunning scamp, a little
camel-boy I have given a silver bit to, and prom-
ised him as much again to keep him for an hour
away from here. Oh! he is a bold little villain,
he will give him a long run across the marsh, and
his bitch meanwhile will keep the *slouguis* busy.
You see, all creatures love; none but you, innocent
dove, refuse the bliss that offers. Be quick! and
as you *will* have the old man to husband spite of
all, I will leave you directly after; and not a soul,
not even the bridegroom on your wedding-night,

will suspect the gentle violence I have done you. I know the secrets they tell young maids, and I will instruct you how they deceive the old."

" I have no wish to deceive anyone .... What secrets will you tell me?"

"Secrets that are only whispered when lips touch lips."

" Well then! begone."

" If you refuse to open, I will lie down across the door, and the old man will stumble over me on his return."

" Oh! no, no! Mansour would kill you! ...."

" He would, and by your fault. For you I will take his blows, like a cringing hound. Oh! to die for you, and leave you the memory of my death! My blood might flow, and I would see it with delight, did I not fear it might fall on your marriage bed. Think, blood, blood that will not be yours, on your wedding couch! Think of me, coming with pale face and breast smeared red, to haunt your first night of love! What! for a word, for one word, one poor little word I would say to you, gazing into your great dark eyes, do you refuse to avert this calamity? I swear it on your head, on mine, on his who to-morrow is to hold you in his arms, Mansour *the Happy* shall through your fault be called Mansour *the Wretched!* The Prophet hears my oath."

" I beseech you, I beseech you, do not poison my life, and the life of the man who has been a loving father to me. What would you say to me? what would you with me?"

"I would love you, love you, love you!"

"Cannot you love me at a distance,—from the other side of the door?"

"A kiss, only one kiss, and I will go at once."

"You swear?"

"By the tomb of the Prophet and the chastisement of God on perjurers!"

XLVI.

SHE opened the door, and he threw himself upon her.

Following an instinctive prompting of modesty, she had extinguished the lamp; she could not bear the first time they met that he should see her face. They were in darkness. She felt his breath burning her cheek, she heard his bosom panting, she was terrified and bewildered at the things he dared and did.

"What are you doing? what do you wish?"

She struggled in his arms, not understanding what he sought, angry and horrified.

"Forgive me! forgive me!" she cried again and again. "What harm have I done you? do not kill me. Why do you hurt me? Help! Mansour, help!"

But he pursued his purpose steadily, profiting by the darkness, and stifling her screams beneath the fury of his kisses.

XLVII.

THEN when the deed was done, he wanted to see her, and so to taste his triumph more completely; and after lighting the lamp, took her in his arms again.

Never in all his travels among the tribes had he encountered a more lovely face, never in all his adventures had he lifted the veil of any daughter of the Hadars so fair, or kissed such entrancing lips, never among all the races of Islam, so rich in beauties, had he seen eyes so dark and flashing. He looked and looked with unflagging admiration, and smiling eyes.

She also looked at him, but her face was without a smile. She was in tears, and visibly afraid. Her heart had been horrified, and was still sad. She was entering life by the gate of sin, and the sight of her lover stirred no feeling but remorse.

"Alas! is *this* love then?" her look seemed to say; but her thoughts were still confused, her mind overwhelmed before the man who had broken so abruptly into the midst of her peaceful life. "What! is this all? Oh! El-Messaoud, El-Messaoud! this then is what you loved me for!" But she was not sure; she did not understand. Why had he left her in such ignorance? If she had known, she would have resisted, she would never have opened the door. He thought he was guarding her purity by keeping her ignorant of evil, and lo! it was this

very purity that had opened wide the door to the
seducer of her honour. She knew now; yes! she
understood now. What would become of her!
And Mansour, why had he not come to her rescue?

All this flashed through her brain in a few seconds.
Then the power of thought left her suddenly. Her
nerves seemed to be paralysed by a keen, biting,
icy wind, though her head was burning. Her heart
almost ceased to beat, and her breast was crushed,
as if a sudden avalanche of horror had buried her.
She felt sick and ill, and her terror grew greater
and greater.

Seeing her so overwhelmed, her seducer shrugged
his shoulders cynically.

" They are all the same," he muttered; " first
they will, and then they won't, and then they will
again, and then, when they have their will, tears
and lamentation! "

And having nothing more to get from her, he
laughed and kissed her on the mouth, and bade
her adieu.

But, as he was re-arranging his girdle, he heard
a hurried step and a moment after a sharp knocking
at the door:

' Afsia," said Mansour's voice, " Afsia, my gazelle,
'tis I."

XLVIII.

HE had come back sooner than Omar expected.
The Spahi had counted on his being away an hour,

and scarcely half that time had elapsed. He was
panting, having returned at topmost speed, urged
by the keenest anxiety.

Yonder amid the black clumps of tall iris a light
of suspicion had broken on his brain.

It was a plot to draw him away from the house!
why of course, his dogs had been purposely enticed
away to a distance from the *haouch* by means of
that confounded bitch. But for what end? for
what end?

At the thought a shiver passed over his head,
as if his shaven crown had been exposed untur-
baned to the North-wind, and he had instantly
turned back, hearing the boy's voice behind him
as he ran sounding like the laugh of some mocking
djinn.

" Have they made a mock of me?" he muttered,
as he ran with all his speed. " Have they made
a mock of me? And who? Why! a child, a mere
child. Oh! the villain!"

He could ejaculate no more, but ran on, spurred
by suspicion.

Then presently, when his limbs failed from fatigue
and he had to resume a quieter pace to recover
breath, he tried to pacify his gnawing anxiety
with such-like soothing thoughts as these:

" Afsia will not open the door, I would stake my life
on it. She is a good and a prudent girl. She will
baulk my enemies' plans. Of course she will not
open to them; how should she? Does she know

14

what evil is? Has her eye ever been sullied by an ill sight? No! no! I am sure of her as I am of myself, nay! surer. And these children of Satan, they shall be mocked at for their pains. God's curse on them and on their designs! may they rot miserably, they and all their generation! Ah! ha! I. have no doubt they are slinking off even now, more shamefaced than Jews who have let themselves be overreached by Christians. Ha! ha! ha! we shall have a fine laugh!"

And he forced himself to laugh, but the sounds that escaped from his dry throat were so dismal and spasmodic they more resembled sobs.

XLIX.

MEANTIME the moon away beyond the bounds of the horizon had shone out clear of her curtain of cloud, like a woman who unrobes and shows her fair body, dazzling beholders with its youthful loveliness. Her orb seemed twice its natural size and flooded the plains with a soft pale light, illuminating the front of the *haouch* and bringing relief to Mansour's spirit. The house looked so calm, so wrapped in peaceful silence, a white pearl in its green encasement of trees, that his heart leapt with joy. He even thought he could distinguish a thin thread of light coming from the window, and said to himself, " She is there! "

At the same moment the breeze, after blowing

over Afsia's garden, reached him laden with the familiar scents, as if her favourite flowers came to greet him with their perfume and confirm his words, saying with him, " She is there! she is there! "

And as the little house grew nearer and nearer and nearer, and showed more and more distinctly through the thick shadows, every trace of anxiety began to vanish from brow and heart. He stopped running, and even began to chide himself for not having gone further to rescue the child. " For perhaps," he thought, " the young villain did really slip into the mud of the marsh." And if that were so, the Sheikh Ben-Kaouaidi and the camel-drivers of the plain would all hold him to be a man of a hard heart and niggard hand.

But he soon consoled himself with the thought that no doubt the boy had found a way out of his dangerous position, and that to-morrow he would send the best of his dogs to the Sheikh.

So after wiping the sweat from his streaming forehead, he went up to the door and knocked, delighted to find it shut.

" Open the door, Afsia, my gazelle, 'tis I."

But the door did not open.

He supposed the girl was asleep, and as he listened for a repetition of a light sound he thought he had caught within, he heard a long way off in the direction of Djenarah the first musket-shots announcing the departure of the wedding-company from the town.

Then he knocked again and louder, repeating again:

"Afsia! Afsia! It is I."

L.

SHE did not stir, or make any attempt to rise. His voice seemed to nail her to the spot. She had only one feeling, a feeling of sick misery and of the violent beating of her heart; so violent was this that her *gandourah* moved up and down, marking its wild throbbing. Her eyes were wide with terror and fixed on the door; to look at her countenance, you would have said the seal that the Unbelievers are marked with, who see not neither do they hear, had just been stamped upon her ears and eyes.

She said to herself, "I am going to die," and lay still, waiting for death. But when Mansour began to redouble his appeals for admittance, at first anxiously, then furiously, she threw an imploring glance at the Spahi, and saw him standing motionless, knitting his heavy brows. Pale as Afsia herself, with eyes fixed on the door, he was drawing slowly from its sheath of red leather one of those long knives with streaked blades that the Khabyle cutlers forge, and which unhitch with one blow the firmest head from the shoulders. He had already searched the room and made sure there was no other issue except the door of the staircase leading to the girl's *oda*. Once there, no further escape was possible, for the two barred windows were barely wide enough for a child's head to pass. He was aware of this; he had studied the *haouch* thoroughly from outside, and knew that in case of surprise, he must needs give battle, and make good his standing, either by force or stratagem. He was not long in coming to a decision, and placing a finger on his lip to command silence, made his way to the staircase, pushed away the *fondouk* and disappeared.

As soon as he was lost in the shadow, Afsia rose painfully, as if the load of shame were already heavy on her shoulders, and crossing the room drew back the bolt.

"Why! what were you doing?" exclaimed Mansour.

"Nothing," she replied.

"Then why did you not open? Why did you not answer? You made my heart black with terror, But you are here! you are here!"

He took her in his arms, and gazed at her with eyes of delight. He could hold her to his breast now; his exertions and anxiety, coupled with the cool freshness of the night, had calmed his senses. He no more felt the same irresistible promptings of desire, and let his lips rest long on the scented tresses.

"Do you know, *tofla?* I have had my race in vain. There's nothing yonder! nothing! I think I have been played with by a miserable little blackguard, who wanted to punish me, because I drove

him away, him and his dog. Ah! but I was afraid
for a moment. Yes! my girl, I was actually afraid
they were coming to carry you off."

And he fondled the thick tresses, took them in
his hand as if to feel their weight, lifted them,
kissed the little wandering curls that escaped over
her bare neck.

She made no resistance, neither speaking nor
hearing, wrapped up in her great terror, trembling
in his arms like a leaf.

"Then just as I was knocking at the door," the
Thaleb whispered softly, "I heard a joyful sound.
Far away in the distance I caught the first musket-
shots of the marriage escort. Our marriage, Afsia!
our marriage!"

But as he gazed into her face, ready to cover it
with kisses, for the first time he noticed her agita-
tion.

"By the head of the Prophet!" he exclaimed.
"My sweet dove, what is wrong?"

"Wrong with me! nothing, Mansour!"

He ran to fetch the lamp, to see her face more
clearly.

"Why! you are pale as though a black *djinn*
had struck you with his wing. Are you ill, my
child? Afsia, dear Afsia, what has happened?"

"I want air. Let me go out of doors. And do
you come with me. I long to hear the sound of the
guns. Come away, let us go meet the horsemen."

Mansour held her back by the arm.

"You are hiding something from me," he cried, filled with sudden suspicion. "Child, I read fear in your eyes as clearly as in a mirror. While I was away, what happened?"

"While you were away ....?" stammered the girl. "Nothing that I know of. I was waiting for you, and I fell asleep."

"And the cold chilled you during your sleep, for you tremble; and now, look! you are too hot, for the fire is blazing in your cheeks. Afsia! Afsia! what does it all mean? Afsia, you cannot be deceiving me!"

LI.

No! she was *not* deceiving him, she could not deceive him, for the truth was plainly legible in her open face and candid eyes. Nevertheless the old *Thaleb*, astute as he was in every wile, could not believe the thing; black suspicion might lodge in the folds of his anxious brow, doubt shudder on the grim abyss of horrid certainty, but he would *not* abandon hope.

"It is impossible," he said again and again; "it cannot be."

Thus it is when we are suddenly confronted by an act of treachery on the part of a dear friend; we cannot at first believe our eyes that see the crime, nor our ears that hear the false words. We say to ourselves. "'Tis a dream," and pinch ourselves to see if we are awake. It seems more possible our senses should be tricked than that our heart should be mistaken; we would rather be victims of hallucination than of roguery. But truth will out. We *have* to believe the evidence; *we* are sane enough, only our heart led us wrong.

Therefore Mansour tried hard to cheat himself, and his thoughts fought desperately against the conclusion forced upon them. He stepped back in order to better scrutinize the girl's face, wishing he could plunge his eyes into her very soul. But she, a child in evil-doing and unskilled at falsehood, kept her eyelids drooped.

"Raise your head," he cried, "show your face, and like a girl whose brow is unsullied with any stain look me in the eye."

She did her best to obey, but her great timid orbs could not meet his fierce glance.

"By God, that sleeps not nor dreams, tell me what has happened."

And seizing her wrists in a grasp that bruised the flesh, he cried with rising anger:

"Daughter of Fathma! By the Lord of Night and Day, answer me! Answer me, what have you done?"

"Let me go," she begged, "do not hurt me!"

"Should I have to break your arms and drive these rings into your flesh, I shall not let you go, till you have told me why you dare not look me in the face."

" Because you frighten me."

" Frighten you!   *I* frighten you!   Since I taught you to stammer your first syllables as a child, and it will be fourteen years ago to-morrow, you have never used that hateful word to me.   Tell me, what are you frightened of?   The guilty only need tremble."

Then looking round the room, he noticed the *fondouk* pushed out of place and the door of the staircase half open.

" Ho! ho! what hand has moved the *fondouk?*"

" I moved it," answered Afsia, whose presence of mind the sense of peril brought back; " I went upstairs to see that nothing had been forgotten; but there was nothing left behind, nothing!"

" You moved it!   God of Heaven!   You!   In the name of woman, that disseminates the seed of Adam, and shakes calamity over our heads like a soiled carpet, you have grown strong in a few hours! Sleep and my absence have been good for you! All the better; I· shall have a sturdy wife, to carry my wallets, if some day poverty drive me to take the road.   But the perfumes your room is still full of penetrate to me here and make my head dizzy; go, shut the door, and push the *fondouk* back into its place, to prevent its opening again."

Afsia went to the door, and exerted all her strength, —but in vain.   Under her little hands the great oaken chest stirred no more than a rock when the evening breeze blows on it.

Returning, she saw Mansour standing with crossed arms and eyes fixed on her face.

"I am tired," she stammered out; "I cannot do it now. No! I cannot do it!"

He continued to look at her, and his pale lips curled with ironical scorn. This is not Mansour her father, Mansour the Kind, Mansour the Happy, but another man altogether, changed beyond recognition, bearing on his face, in his eyes jaundiced by passion, in the spasmodic contraction of his cheeks, the signs of an implacable anger.

Then in confusion and terror she drew back to the wall with hands clasped before her, and whispered:

"Forgive me!"

"Forgive!" he repeated after her in hollow tones. "You ask forgiveness! But what am I to forgive? I do not know the crime you have committed.... you dare not tell me what it is. Is it so shameful you blush to confess?.... Well, then! I am going to find it out for myself; for I begin to understand.... yes! I see the truth."

LII.

As easily as though he were lifting a sheaf of corn, he laid her over his left arm, tearing off her girdle, and the *foutah* and silk drawers she wore. Then raising the vest of gauze that clung to her sides, he tossed it back over her head, as the shroud is thrown over a dead face.

And her shuddering body was exposed, naked from the breasts to the ankles.

Then he could plainly see the stains of outrage on her.

Without a word, he pushed the unhappy girl roughly from him, put his hand to his head, and reeled staggering against the wall. He looked like a man who has received a heavy blow on the head; but it was only his heart that was wounded,—a wound that stunned him.

But remembering his rival was there, no doubt jeering and exulting in his success, he stiffened his limbs to resist the agony. His pride of strength, his former vigour, the memory of past prowess, he appealed to them all to help him struggle against the present; and wound up like some powerful engine, every spring of his nerves drawn tight, he broke into a loud laugh, that was more like a cry of pain.

He had uttered the same laugh, when he was crossing the plain and first felt assured of his calamity. It was the tears he strove to keep back, the groans he was fain to stifle, that escaped in this laughter that was a sob.

He resolved to be more calm; and in the slow, subdued accents of a man pondering and talking to himself, he spoke over Afsia's head, where she lay crouching on the ground, in the same attitude as when she fell, hiding her face and her shame in her arms.

"It is all over," he muttered, "all over now! What is done cannot be undone. I would fain forget, but I cannot. I would fain forgive, but it is impossible. I would close the wound, if I could, but the scar would be there for ever. By the Prophet of God, 'tis the chastisement of Mansour."

"One evening, alone, worn out and weary, I said, 'Enough! enough! Dissipation confuses the mind, but it does not bring forgetfulness; intoxication once past, memory comes back again; and I, I must bury all my past in one woman's heart.' I sought her from North to South, from the setting sun to the dawn. For the loved one must not trail behind her, like myself, a stain to darken all her life, no blot must dim the brightness of her days, no regretful memories sadden her, no remorse for a broken, unhappy past torment her peace, the starry purity of her eyes must be the beacon of my future; I must have a virgin bride! .... And so one day of madness I adopted a new-born babe; I took her from her mother's womb, to make sure of her unsullied purity. And from that day I have never left her; for fourteen years I have watched over her. Not a thought of hers I have not shared; not a gesture I have not followed; not a word I have not heard. And when after fourteen years' waiting, I was to enjoy the woman I had earned by all my care and self-sacrifice and love, when she was yet pure as Eve before Adam implanted in her side the accursed race of mankind, a moment,

one moment that my eye was not upon her, was
enough for her undoing; I left her a maid, I come
back to find her, what? . . . . What? . . . . How
did it come about? . . . . She had none of the
morbid longings that torment the young and urge
them to fly the happy paternal roof, and to seek
in the perilous unknown another roof and another
life. No stain had as yet sullied her thoughts.
Her innocence was complete, and she knew no
difference between the daughters and the sons
of Adam! A rose-bud! A flower half opened
to the dawn, that no breath of evil has blighted!
A maid immaculate, unconscious what maidenhood
means! And now! All over! all over! An instant
and the ruin is accomplished! the rose-bud sullied!
the flower withered! A filthy grub has fouled the
blossom. Some drunken hog has wallowed on the
rose! My *houri* has been the victim of his lewd
abominations. Under my eyes! under my very eyes,
while a child, his hireling, played on my simplicity,
a coward villain has robbed me of my joy, my
honour, my happiness, my future, robbed me of my
life; and in place of the human wonder I had reared,
of my *houri* of Paradise, of my virgin-bride, he
leaves me a harlot!"

And as he went on, his calmness began to leave
him again, and his anger to rise again to fever heat.

"A harlot! a harlot, lying, and cheating, and
then hiding her face behind the mask of sham
repentance. Bitch, and child of a bitch, get up!"

he shouted, and pushed her with his foot; "how long have you been deceiving me? Where did you see him first? What devilish ingenuity did you find to make your barefaced lies invisible to my eyes? How much did he pay you for your shame, the thief that lurks up yonder, the cowardly dog who has ruined your good-name and robbed me of my honour? For there he is, you know he is! There he is, and I am going to kill him, and my dogs shall tear his dead body limb from limb. Ha! ha! a treat for my *slouguis!* Up, brave dogs, up! At him! at him!"

Then he took down his long fighting musket, hanging on the wall all ready loaded for the *feu de joie* that was to greet the wedding.

LIII.

AESTA had not quailed under Mansour's insults, and even when he kicked her, she still cowered at his feet. But hearing the click of the musket, she sprang up and leapt upon him.

"Do not kill him," she cried, "oh! do not kill him! I beseech you not to kill him!"

She leant all her weight on his breast, struggling to grasp the gun, and gazing eagerly, all shame forgotten, with terror and supplication into his fierce, hard eyes.

"Ah! ha! so you are afraid for his life."

"Kill me. *I* opened the door; *I* waved my haïk,

and he thought he was bound to come. Kill me;
I am to blame, it was all my fault. Oh! if you
ever loved me, kill me."

He looked keenly at her, and his eyes blazed
with a fierce light.

"How you love him!" he exclaimed.

"No! I do not love him! I do not know him;
but *I* am to blame, and I beseech you not to kill
him."

"You to blame! You! *Allah Kebir! Allah Kebir!*
It was written. The head of the mighty is bowed
beneath the implacable hand of fate. Old men told
me in the days of my youth, 'Soul for soul, eye for
eye, tooth for tooth, wound for wound.' And the
wounds of the heart count double; for they are
incurable. Yes! it was the heart I wounded in old
days, and lo! I am punished. It is just. Have no
fear for the man's life. I promised him his life
fourteen years ago, I swore it over your cradle.
By the grave that gapes at the end of the road of
human life, by the grave where we shall all one
day lie, great and small, happy and wretched,
robbers and robbed, fortune that has flattered too
long, lies hard on me to-day. She confronts me
with my master, she has set up in my path to
baulk me one that is more cunning and a stronger
man than I. I must bow down before him,—yes!
I know my duty,—and call him Lord!"

And suddenly pushing the girl aside:

"Ho! there above," he shouted, "man, lover,

djinn, devil, be you what you may, come down, and show your slave the face of his Lord."

A moment's silence followed. At length a slow step made itself heard, and Omar pushing open the door with his foot, appeared in the dim opening, dagger in hand.

LIV.

THE looks of the old and the young man crossed like two sword-blades. The hand of each gripped his weapon firmer, but the old man presently dropped the butt of his musket to the floor.

"Come nearer, come a step nearer; I would see your face. And you, *tofla*, back! Ah! I have seen you before once; I remember you, and my remembrance is unfavourable. Come forward, have no fear. By the glorious Koran! by the holy Caaba stone! by the star at its setting! by the sovereign Lord of the East and of the West! I swear; you may put up your *flissa* in its sheath."

"Do you take me for a madman or a fool; do you think I shall stand unarmed to face your wrath?"

"You are distrustful, and that shows you are untrustworthy. In the young suspicion is a sure sign of a base heart. O Afsia! Afsia! what a man you have given yourself to! However what I have said is said. When I was your age, young sir, I thought to conquer fate when I entered on the road

of evil, but fate has conquered me. Fate makes
me your plaything. But spite of my degradation,
I am of those whose word is to be trusted. Look,
I lay my weapon here. And now, my master, tell
me by what name I am to greet you."

"I desired to ask you that very question," replied
the soldier haughtily, "for I am called Omar simply,
Omar—without father's name; but Lagdar-ben-El-
Arbi, the merchant, of the *Ksour* of Msilah, informs
me you can tell me more,—and you alone."

Mansour raised his two arms above his head:

"Lagdar! Lagdar-ben-El-Arbi! It is he that sends
you here! he that advised your coming! Ah! I
understand, I understand. Oh! Meryem! Meryem!"

"My mother's name!" exclaimed the Spahi. "Why
do you invoke her name? Is there aught in com-
mon betwixt you and her? I remember as a child
how my boyish comrades, who every one had a
father, used to laugh in my face and cry that name
at me, adding another, *Cabah* (prostitute). I used
to thrash them, but they all leagued together against
me, and shouted louder than ever *Ben-Cabah!*
Ben-Cabah! harlot's son! harlot's son! They in-
sulted me, and thrashed me too. This injustice of my
childish companions disgusted and enraged me, but
I have learned since man's justice is no better!
Do you hear,—Meryem, called *Cabah!* Cabah!
My mother with her gentle face and modest eyes!
My mother driven out with her son into the desert,
as they teach us Hadjira (Hagar) was of old by

15

the wicked Ibrahim (Abraham); my mother wandering the roads without a shelter for her head; my mother dead in wretchedness and disgrace. Tell me, by whose fault? by whose wickedness? Why do you gaze at me, as though you saw the face of a phantom? Speak! speak! Ah! when men still named you Mansour *the Happy*, the tale of your insolent success and your bold intrigues came to the ears of a boy who himself had a by-name too—Omar *the Devil's Child!*"

Mansour would have spoken, but his tongue refused its office. His throat was dry, and his eyes ready to overflow. He extended his arm towards the son of Meryem, and a tear coursed down his furrowed cheek.

"Answer me," persisted Omar, "answer, is it true you can tell me the name of my father?"

"Son of *Meryem-ben-El-Ketib*," at length the *Thaleb* replied in a hollow voice, "if you know your father's name, why ask me for it? If you do not know it, learn it is for ever dishonoured, and you are better to remain in ignorance. Go in peace; return to the man who sent you, to Lagdar the merchant, and tell him he is . . . . avenged."

"I will do as you wish. But I would hear first from your lips the name of the man who was my father, and Meryem's . . . lover."

"You hurt me by insisting. Surely I have had enough humiliations for one day! Why must you know the name?"

"That I may curse it!"

Mansour bowed his head. Then suddenly drawing himself up, he looked his son in the face and said:

"Listen! I see by your words and still more by the fire in your eyes that you know the truth. You are right, you owe me nothing but hatred. He who sows tares must only count on a harvest of tares.

"Now hear me. The girl you see yonder in tears, listening in terror as the curtain is rent that I had set up between her and the foul brutalities of life, is the loveliest flower of the plain, and never in all the land from the one sea with its blue waves to the other that rolls its grey billows of sand beyond the palms, never have True Believers or Giaours seen the match of her wondrous beauty. You have stained her purity, and you can efface the stain. Take her! she is yours. Giving her you of my own free will, I pay every debt I could ever have owed to Meryem's son. Farewell!"

So saying, he dropped his wild, sad eyes, and sank on the rush mat. Then unfastening from his neck his ivory rosary, the sole relic of his father he possessed, he began to tell the beads with a feverish hand, muttering hoarsely, "*Allah Kebir! Allah Kebir! Allah Kebir!*" By this means he endeavoured to still the tumult of his thoughts and be deaf to the agony of his spirit.

His tone of utter misery pierced Afsia to the heart, and she threw herself at his feet and besought him:

"Keep me with you! keep me! I cannot go with him. Let me stay here; I will be your servant... simply your servant, Mansour."

But he wrapped himself up in his sorrow as in a rugged outer shell, against which her sobs battered in vain:

"Away with you," he said savagely, "what is done, is done; what is spoken, is spoken. Tears may wash out a fault, they are unavailing against an insult. Begone!"

Then turning his gaze within, refusing to see anything, or hear anything more, he drew down the hood of his *burnouse* over his head, and began again in a loud voice:

"*Allah Kebir! Allah Kebir! Allah Kebir!*"

Omar smiled, and seizing the girl by the arm, drew her outside.

"Come," he said, "as he turns you out!"

But at the threshold she stopped, and throwing a heart-broken look on Mansour, who was determined not to share his grief with any, on the room that for so many years had been brightened by her youth and gaiety, she was seized with anguish, and clinging to the door with her little hand which had remained free, she cried: "Mansour! Mansour!"

But he never stirred, but kept on repeating his appeal to heaven:

"*Allah Kebir! Allah Kebir! Allah Kebir!*"

LV.

MANSOUR heard the sound of footsteps gradually dying away in the night, then when all was still, he raised his head; it was the countenance of an old man the lamp that stood before him revealed. Sudden grief had torn away his mask of apparent manliness, and of the strong man of former days nothing was left but the gloomy light that burned in his eye,—last glimmer of the dying fire. *There* was concentrated all the surviving vigour of his dying soul.

He looked round the empty room, as if surprised to find it so, then he essayed to rise; but his limbs bent under him, and he fell back heavily on the mat.

"What! what! am I so old as that?" he cried, laughing harshly. "Ah! ha! what a fine bridegroom!"

This word, bridegroom, was like the lash of a whip to the old man: he dragged himself to the door and listened. But he heard no sound of what he longed to hear,—the footfall of her he had loved so well.

"Gone!" he said to himself, "gone! Can it be? Afsia gone; and *I* drove her away, and I shall never see her more. I have heard the sound of her step for the last time, her step that made my heart laugh within me, and her voice that sang in my soul. I shall never hear her voice, her soft,

sweet voice, again! Afsia, my milk-white gazelle!
And I, I drove her away! Why did she not tarry
a minute? Why did she not turn once again to
cover my hand with her tears? I should have
forgiven everything. Yes! I was ready to forgive
her everything, spite of his being there and his
mockery. But she consented, she wished, to follow
him; she let him drag her roughly away, without
a word of protest, without an attempt to return;
she was in a moment his humble servant, as if he
possessed any other right over her but that of having
ravished and seduced her; she cried at the door,
Mansour! Mansour—and that was all! Ah! if she
would return, if she would escape from him, if she
came running to me, crying Mansour! Mansour!
again,—there is yet time—how I would open my
arms wide to welcome her! I would make him
fight for her! What care I for her defilement! I
would wash it clean, I would make it as though it
had never been, I would drown it in the ocean of
my love. What care I who put on her the defile-
ment! I do not know him. How do I know he
speaks truth? Son of Meryem! but I do not know
him; I *will* not know him. I know none but
Afsia! Afsia! Afsia!"

He listened, but his cry found no echo. There
was no answer, except a confused tumult towards
Djenarah of men's voices and horses' feet.

"Then the others who are drawing near," he
cried, "coming with their inopportune gaiety and

insolent congratulations. Oh! I cannot bear it; I
will not bear it. Strong men force even calamity
to give way before them, and snap like a bit of
wood the evil spell the *djenouns* cast on them. I
am strong, as strong as any, and for more than
thirty years men have named me *the Happy*.

He reached out his arm and grasped once more
his long fighting gun, the *moukhalah* that never
missed, then shaking his stiffened limbs, he felt all
the vigour of the young circulating again in his
veins, and darted out into the darkness.

"Son of Meryem!" he shouted, "'tis war to the
death between us!"

LVI.

HE directed his course across the plain, following
the same path he had traversed an hour before,
when hard driven by the clamouring of his excited
senses he had rushed away, fearing to continue longer
in the perilous neighbourhood of his bride.

Ah! he would have done better to forget his
oaths, to have made light of ridicule, to have robbed
himself of his own treasure. Then she would not
be going away with another, tramping the highroads
by night!

He started for the marsh at a run. This is the
way they would naturally have taken, fugitives and
ashamed, to avoid the wedding-guests.

Soon in fact he perceived the two shadowy forms

advancing slowly through the long grass. He could see their heads, and from time to time the man's bent down to the woman's.

"Stop!" he shouted panting, for he was exhausted with running, "stop, thief, you who are stealing my bride from me."

"Your bride belongs to me," retorted the other. "What! have you thought better of it? would you take her back again? Ah! the folk of Djenarah have told me true, when they said you had no scruples, and how in the days of your youth you sought a mistress in your father's bed. But you are mistaken, old man, if you think I will consent to give up the fair child to glut your senile lust."

At this insult Mansour's eyes flashed a ruddy fire, as they had done in hours of combat when he cried to the warriors of his *goum*:

"Forward, my lads, forward; and strike home! It is not lead that kills, but fate."

And he brought his gun to his shoulder:

"Afsia!" he cried, stoop down."

But it was only a momentary flash; he grounded his musket again, and merely said:

"You who slunk into a house that before your coming was peaceful and happy, and quitted it leaving behind you darkness and death, forget my name, as I forget yours. Forget it till the day that chastisement shall burst in at your door, and enter beneath your roof even as you entered under mine. Then you will remember your father, *Mansour-ben-Ahmed.*"

"You have said the word yourself, I owe you nothing," returned the other. "The curse you threaten me with fall back on your own head!"

"O son of Meryem, I curse you not. The Prophet keep me from the deed; enough surely that my own head is doomed. But hearken to my advice, or rather my supplication. May she you take with you never, never have a heavy hour. Wrap her warm in happiness and love."

Presently, his voice softening in spite of himself, he said:

"And you, Afsia! you carry my life with you; I have no right now to keep you. Beside your life, full of hope, mine that has nought but desolation and despair must not weigh in the balance. But I am afraid for you, I am sore afraid you are going to an evil fate, with evil for your yokefellow. Hearken, my child! hearken to my last words. If ever calamity should come upon you, remember, remember there is a spot in the wide plain, far from sultans, far from wicked, jealous men, where a *haouch*, your own home, will await you, in darkness and gloom, till you return to bring back its sunshine. The door shall stand ever open for you; come by day, if you can unashamed; come by night, if you dread men's eyes; come clad in festal robes, or covered with infamy and wearing the rags of poverty; come, accursed of men and abandoned of God; the old man will be there to welcome you,—the man who was to have been your husband, who should have been content to remain only your father—he will welcome you, and till his last hour keep a place for you at his fireside, a place for you in his heart. And now one word of farewell: Go in peace! in peace! in peace!"

He listened to know if she made him any answer, if she cried farewell to him, but he heard nothing. Then he fell to his knees and laid his forehead to the ground, wetting the dust with his tears.

Dragged away by a pitiless arm, Afsia was compelled to follow; and when, touched to the heart by the sad, sad voice, she strove to turn back and cry: "Mansour! Mansour, I am here!" her ruthless lover put a hand over her mouth, and pushing her before him said brutally, "On with you! on!"

So she went on her way, sobbing. She went on till she heard her name three times repeated in the gloom:

"Afsia! Afsia! Afsia!"

Then she fell fainting in the road.

LVII.

MEANTIME the wedding-guests were approaching, a merry, noisy band.

Young and old were on horseback, and the Caïd headed the procession. To do honour to his brother, he had summoned the Sheikhs of the whole neighbourhood to the ceremony; and they and all their followers were there, musket on thigh, pricking

with their long spurs or with the sharp angle of
the stirrup the prancing stallions and fiery mares,
that wild with excitement and with smoking nostrils,
curvetted and champed the bit, impatient to be
started in the brilliant cavalcade.

For now they were drawing near the *haouch*; it
could be made out bathed in the first beams of the
coming day, cradled in the greenery of its oasis.

"Gallop! gallop, sons of the plain! put your
coursers to the gallop! Now is the time to display
your strength and skill, to show before the fairest
eyes in all the *Souf* how well the children of the
desert can wield a musket and bestride a horse.

"For Afsia, the beauteous Afsia, the old *Thaleb's*
bride, will look on all with her great eyes soft as
the gazelle's; who knows but she may remark one
of you? Then to-night, in the arms of her white-
haired bridegroom, the remembrance of the young
horseman will perchance cross her mind, and she
will think: "Why is he not at my side in this old
man's place?" And to be there in her thoughts,
though invisible, a third at the feast of love that
night, is it not one step towards winning her heart
some day?

"Gallop! sons of the plain, gallop! To-day is no
day to spare your powder. Up, guns! and fire!"

And long and loud the musketry rang out, tearing
to tatters with its merry crash and rattle the deep
silence of the valley.

Then all dashed forward at the gallop.

LVIII.

" GALLOP! gallop!" And like a company of *djenouns*, they swept by in wild tumultuous career, shaking the very ground beneath their feet.

" Gallop! gallop! sons of the desert! Ho! *Thaleb! Thaleb-El-Messaoud!* All hail to you! All blessings on your head! The *Happy Man!* the *Happy Man!* Glory and honour to the *Happy Man* and his bride!"

So young and old, women and girls mounted on mules and raising shrill *staccato* cheers, *krammés* that ran behind, the negress Mabrouka witnessing her delight by screams of laughter, the bridegroom's stallion, great-grandson of Naama the beautiful, ready bridled, with trappings of red leather broidered with gold, the Caïd's wedding-gift, the white mule caparison'd in gold and silk destined for the bride, —all sped by like a flash of lightning.

But crouching in the tall grass of the narrow sunken way, a man white-bearded and fierce-eyed, cowering there like some evil beast, elbows on knees, his chin supported by his clenched fists, watched them pass.

And fifty paces behind the cavalcade, he saw on a grey mule like that which once in old days had carried the daughter of the *Muezzin* El-Ketib over the desert sands, a fat man with a red, mocking face, whom he recognized as the merchant Lagdar-ben-El-Arbi, once the lover of Meryem.

And the song-birds awoke and flooded the neigh-
bouring thickets with their first merry notes to
greet the dawn, the water-fowl clapped their wings,
and the lark, soaring high in the morning air,
poured out his joyous song:

> Oh! merry time,
> When lovers meet
> Among the wheat,
> In summer's prime!

LIX.

LOUD was the laughter throughout the town, and
Mansour's enemies went about crying in the streets
and in the market-place: "The chastisement of
Mansour! the chastisement of Mansour!"

The *Caïd* was ashamed of his brother's conduct,
and forbade his name to be mentioned in his presence.

As for Mansour himself, he was seen no more
in public.

And from that day forth the *haouch* in the plain
of Ain-Chabrou lies desolate, mournful as a grave
awaiting its occupant. Yet just as of old, the sun
kisses it lovingly, the green oasis blooms around,
the birds break into song, and the brook runs bab-
bling under the poplars. But tall weeds have in-
vaded the threshold; leprous patches of moss eat into
the cracked walls, the roof has fallen in and lets
the winter rains come through, and the door battered
down one stormy night, hangs half broken by one

of its twisted hinges. In Afsia's chamber, great brown spiders spread their treacherous webs in every corner, and snakes nest on the bed where once she slept.

Sometimes on dark nights dismal outcries are heard, mingling with the howls of starving dogs and the jackals' yelping. No man dares approach, for the camel-drivers of the plain declare the place haunted by Eblis the Damned. But indeed it is only Mansour the Damned dwells there, and pays Fate the price of the thirty years when men surnamed him *the Happy Man !*

The sounds heard are his groans and cries, when driven by sleeplessness from his mat of rotting cane, he wanders forth along the gloomy tracks that traverse the swamp. He is old and mad, and thinks his bride will come back some day; so he calls her name, and waits, waits for one that never comes.

But neither he nor the folk of Djenarah, neither the goat-herds of the mountain nor the camel-men of the plain, nor yet the herdsmen of the valley, have ever again seen her they knew under the names of *Sidi-Messaoud's bride* and the *Maid of Ain-Chabrou.*

EPILOGUE

ONE hot afternoon the lieutenant *Omar-bou-Skin* took his seat on a stone bench under the arcade of *Dar-el-Bey*.

The horses belonging to the squadron of Constantine had gone to the river to water, and he was waiting for their return, meantime humming over some of his favourite couplets:

> Her lips are a cup of pleasure,
> Brimmed full of blood-red wine;
> Pressed to her bosom's treasure,
> To die were bliss divine,
> With Kreïra,
> Fair Kreïra,
> With Kreïra, were she mine, were she mine,—
> Were she mine, the rose of Ouargla!

He was to marry on the morrow a little maid of twelve, sweet as a dream of love, whom he had bought for two hundred *douros*; and he felt gay and happy at the prospect.

At this moment an Arab woman, wrapped in an elegant *moulaïa* of fine linen and wearing the white stockings, neat and close gartered, that ladies of pleasure affect, approached slowly.

The officer looked at her smiling, for she had great gazelle-like eyes, limpid at once and flashing, and beneath the folds of her *haïk* you could see lurked youth and beauty.

When she was near him, she stopped and her eyes darted fire.

He still smiled, but suddenly the smile froze on his lips; the woman had drawn aside her veil.

"What! you," he said, turning pale, almost as if he were afraid.... "what would you with me?"

He made a movement to rise, but fell back heavily on the stone seat. The wooden hilt of a long Khabyle dagger planted in his breast stood out below his neck.

He opened his mouth to cry out, and a single syllable, three times repeated, escaped his lips like a death-rattle:

"Af.... Af.... Af...."

The blood that spouted in a torrent from his throat bore the rest away into the silence of eternity.

Deadly pale and with haggard eyes, the woman bent a few seconds over his drooping head, then coldly said:

"He is dead! It was written! Mansour is avenged!"

The Spahis of the guard rushed at her furiously, some of them with clenched and uplifted fists, but seeing her so fair, no one struck her.

She never spoke a word, and suffered them to lead her away quite unresisting. To the questions of the French judge and even to those of the *Cadi* she opposed an obstinate silence.

All that came to light at the enquiry was that she had long been the favourite mistress of the lieutenant Omar-bou-Skin, and that she was well known to the officers under the name of *Meryem*.

They shot her one May morning, in a quiet business-like way, on a piece of waste-land to the south of Constantine near the road that leads to the Land of Palms.

Allah Kebir! Allah Kebir! Allah Kebir!

THE END.

16

POSTSCRIPT

Πάντα μὲν καθαρὰ τοῖς καθαροῖς· τοῖς δὲ
μεμιασμένοις καί ἀπίστοις οὐδὲν καθαρὸν, ἀλλα
μεμίανται αὐτῶν καὶ ὁ νοῦς καὶ ἡ συνέιδησις.

(TITUS, Ch. I, 15)

POSTSCRIPT

As long ago as 1880, seventeen years since, the present Book, the whole of which was written in England, appeared for the first time in print, being published in Paris by Alphonse Lemerre. In 1885 an *edition de luxe* was brought out in London; and later on several popular editions were issued one after the other by the two Parisian publishers Edinger, and Fayard.

The London edition, of which a number of copies were sent to the press by the Publisher, MARTIN HUBERT, did not fail to excite cries of protest from the horde of hypocrits and prudes always so numerous. A weekly Review bearing the curious title of "The Bat", a name it presumably deserved, declared the book the APOTHEOSIS OF RAPE WITH VIOLENCE, and called for the intervention of the Public Prosecutor! However, common sense still exists, thank God, in Great Britain; there are still to be found in that country men of enlightenment, neither blinded by a ridiculous prudishness nor driven imbecile by the cant of a hypocritical and intolerant religion. Such men recognize the high morality of the work, of which a Publisher, as open-minded as he is learned, now issues this edition for the first time in English.

The Book fell by chance into the hands of Mr. Charles Carrington, who was pleased with the style, and saw at once the philosophic range of the Work. The Publisher in question is far from being an ordinary man; he is a scholar and a distinguished Orientalist, one who possesses an intimate acquaintance not only with the languages of Asia but with those of Europe as well. His extensive travels and wide learning, which place him in a position very far above the average, have inspired him with the healthy and hearty scorn *Alceste* speaks of in the play, for the fanatics of so-called purity, for the stern-faced moralists whose panoply of virtue covers the most horrid vices. 1

How well we know them, the folk who veil their faces in consternation before a work of Art, because it displays undraped the glories of the human form divine! How well we know them, the folk who in public profess themselves shocked to hear the word, and all the while in secret delight to do the thing,—like old maids over their tea, blushing at the very mention of such a dreadful word as *chemise*, but regaling their prurient imaginations with the pictures of passion certain chapters of the Bible present, and licking their lips over the *Song of Solomon!* But England has no monopoly of such-like oddities. "Their name is Legion" in *godfearing* Germany as it is in *immoral* France. The tribe of *Tartufes* is just as much alive and to the fore now as it was in Molière's time, and his:

"Cachez ce sein que je ne saurais voir,"

is quite in the modern taste.

The very same hypocrisy that Molière ridiculed spreads

1 The editor is pleased to see Captain France has so good an opinion of him though he does not personally feel worthy of it.

over the texture of our lives like an oil-stain, thanks to the active propaganda of a class of *Gérontes* who once more justify and more than justify the old proverb, "When the Devil grew old, the Devil a monk would be". But above all others it is those Puritan critics who are offended by plain. speaking, by the *mot propre*, that we have a right to call ridiculous and absurd.

In former days Pierre Bayle discussed solemnly in his learned *Dictionary* how the fact that a girl was with child could be stated before *a highly respectable woman*, without wounding her modesty. "The latter could be told:—*She has had the misfortune to become pregnant;—Some one has taken advantage of her;—He has kept company with her;— They have known each other too well;—They have had inter- course together;—He has enjoyed the greatest favour a woman can give;—She has yielded him her most precious possession; the consequences show it;—What has passed between them cannot be mentioned in decent terms, ears polite would not tolerate it;—Her honour is flawed, it is in want of repairs."* How perfectly idiotic all this is!

Then the worthy Bayle goes on: "A number of other phrases might be found still better veiled; in which to reply to the *respectable woman's* question; but each and all of them would but serve to depict to her mind's eye, as vigorously as Michael Angelo could have done on canvass, the *foul and bestial action* that resulted in the girl's pregnancy."

So, the act which perpetuates the human race, the act to which we are all indebted for our existence, the union of the sexes, the supreme consecration of Love, is a foul and bestial action! We are to blush at Nature's methods, the methods by which we have been procreated. Bayle's "*respectable lady*" would fall fainting to the floor, if she were told plainly: "The girl is with child, as your own mother was before you were born, as your grandmother was before she brought your mother into the world, as were all your female ancestors before you one after the other down the centuries, from your first mother Eve, who was impregnated by your first father Adam; as you yourself, 'respectable lady', were by your husband before you bore your daughters, who too will be impregnated in their turn."

It must be a dream; and you ask yourself in amazement, Have these good people then utterly lost *all* common sense? For if you will think a moment, they make out the Supreme Being, God the Creator, to be the father of all immorality.

Well! well! we can only cry to Him from the depths: "Lord! Lord! have pity on the fools, for they know not what they say,—though they know very well what they do!"

HECTOR FRANCE.

PARIS, December 1897.

L'AMOUR AU PAYS BLEU.

Journal du Dimanche (Supplément de l'Europe).

(Brussels, Jan. 16. 1881.)

I have had occasion more than once before to express the admiration I feel for the talent of Hector France. He is one of the few writers of real worth who are free from the trammels of any school and march straight along their own road, drawing solely and entirely on their own impressions.

In one word, he possesses style,—and the style is his own, a quite distinctive combination of elegance and vigour. Readers will remember the rugged charm of his earlier Novel, the terrible story of the "Homme qui tue", which first revealed his talents as a narrator and a poet, and yet how at the same time the horrors of the tale were relieved by touches of tender and delicate feeling. The fact is that his very special grasp of the conditions of the Romance enabled him to frame his narrative of murder in a setting of beautiful scenery, and mitigate the sacrifice of life by the splendour of natural surroundings.

A constitutional bent indeed inclines him to the dramatic,—soon as ever he touches humanity, his matter grows terrifying; yet ever and anon he seems to feel a dread of going too far in this direction, and instantly the wide peace of Nature succeeds the fierce passions of his characters. The critic who should make a more prolonged study of his books would find himself in contact with a mind at once simple-hearted and corrupted, a soul still virgin through all the stress and strain of thought, a man in whom familiarity with the darkest phases of reality has not killed the ideal.

The present book is a proof of this. I know no narrative bearing in a higher degree than this the double character of mocking cynicism and youthful unspoiled poetry. It gives off a perilous, heady perfume, the intoxicating reflection of a Paradise of love that momently falls in unexpected ruin, and leaves you disappointed and disillusioned face to face with the most bestial of actualities. Once more in the pages before us, rending the veil of tears and sentiment and romantic love, the human animal breaks his chain; the savage monster appears, sacrificing all to his furious desires; and in red streams the blood crawls over the fair face of the landscapes the Author depicts. It is the "Songs of Songs" of rape and violation.

For the rest, nothing can be imagined more truly Oriental, in matter and in form, than "The Chastisement of Mansour",—nowhere a trace of the cold, calculating man of the North; the language, richly ornamented yet carefully wrought, preserves even in descriptive passages the glittering precision of the sonnet. You admire the feat, you appreciate the high literary merit; but you cannot help some feeling of regret that so precious a gift of style is not employed on less exotic subjects. Further, the characters are boldly drawn, in broad outlines, free from all unnecessary detail; and Mansour in his hard fierce senile concupiscence possesses even a certain tragic grandeur that puts him on a pedestal apart among the heroes of Fiction. A true work of art, the child of a rich and fervid imagination, teeming with exquisite bits of description, it leaves behind in the fancy a vague yearning after vanished hours of love and doom.

CAMILLE LEMONNIER.

Le Soleil (Nov. 15th, 1880.)

It must not be forgotten that we are here in the land of Islam, where manners are of a kind to soften considerably some of the colours that might seem to us too crude. Is it not a strange thing to find a writer of such powers,—it is not too much to say, a poet,—showing himself so careless of his high talent as to consent to put his name below some of those "feuilletons" that fill up the bottom of the page in certain journals, mere weapons of party warfare, lacking equally sincerity and honesty, that pervert the popular imagination by the display of pictures of life arbitrarily invented to serve the ends of the fiercest political passions? Among the mass of novels of which I select only the quintessence for mention here, this book of M. Hector France's stands out conspicuous by its originality and the real charm of the form wherewith he clothes the brilliant colouring and ardent blaze of the "Pays Bleu", that is to say Algeria, —a land where men's passions are as hot as the climate with its unbroken sunlight, and where they cull women like flowers, just budding on the stem.

CH. CANIVET.

Courrier du Soir (Nov. 28th, 1880.)

In Algeria passions are turbulent, and love a fiery furnace; if we were not aware of this before, M. Hector France's book would teach us the fact. Rugged manners, impetuous characters, heart-stirring scenes, this book offers us on every page. Some of the pictures have a brutal colouring, altogether primitive in its tones, of which the Bible affords us the only other example. Such is life in the desert, in that "Pays Bleu", where M. Hector France takes us.

. . . .
The motive is dramatic, the tendency of the work severely moral. M. Hector France has worked out his subject as a writer who knows Algeria thoroughly and loves it deeply. He does not speak like a cold-blooded man of the West; his style takes on a rich Eastern colouring and in very truth he offers his readers some very striking descriptions.

The tale is a kind of pastoral; at times you seem to be perusing the scenes of an exuberant, barbarous eclogue. The handling may be heavy, but a rugged poetry results from more than one of the pictures drawn. Very likely the book could hardly have been written otherwise, so as to seem real to us. The story is told in such a way as to force the attention; it is stirring and full of passion. In the days we live in, its very defects will serve to call the notice of the public to the work.]

ANTONY VALABREQUE.

Le Livre (December 1880).

"The Chastisement of Mansour" (L'Amour au Pays Bleu) is a book bathed in sunlight, warm and living. In the pictures M. France draws us with his master hand, we have at one and the same time the colouring of a Fromentin and the poetry of a Gérome. This most original novel shows us Oriental fatalism in a convincing way ..... A superb canvas, admirably wrought with arabesques of infinite variety and infinite skill. Read the book; it is one for connoisseurs.

OCTAVE UZANNE.

République Française (Jan. 17th, 1881).

There is much that is both strange and picturesque, much prose,—even realistic prose, but at the same time a vein of rich poetry, in this story of an Arab Don Juan, a debauchee, an habitual seducer of married women and unmarried, to whom the idea occurs one day, as it does to Molière's Arnolphe, to bring up an Agnes from the cradle, in order to make her his wife later, incontestably virgin in body and mind. Young love, in this case too, thwarts the schemes of the old roué, and the vengeance of his former victims rises up suddenly before him. The painting of the private life of this fair corner of Algeria, the "Pays Bleu", has a new and quite original character of its own. The landscape is at once familiar and almost a lyric. The flavour of this unique book cannot be better defined than by saying it reminds one at one and the same time of the "Dernier des Abencerages" and of "Madame Bovary". The combination is quite novel; but unity of impression and the stamp of truth are there none the less.

FABRICE W.

Le Panthéon de l'Industrie (Nov. 14th, 1897).

This is a charming and original work, a Romance of Algerian life, wild and poetical, the style half Biblical, half modern, highly wrought and very picturesque.
It is the story of a debauchee, Mansour, a kind of Arab Don Juan, who after having seduced the fair Meryem, his own father's young wife, pursues the ideal of love down to old age, when finally he adopts a child, the little Afsia, whose maidenhood he reserves for himself ....

The whole narrative, written more in the manner of a poem than of an ordinary novel, is intermingled with the most delightful descriptions, sometimes a trifle free, but the boldness of which is veiled under a certain Oriental mysticism that makes them full of charm.

In any case literature of the sort, all ideal in its aims, is preferable to the flat, nauseating productions of the realistic school.

C. GEORGE.

Le Républicain de Tarn· et Garonne (Dec. 19th, 1880).

..... The "Pays Bleu" M. Hector France tells us of is not the land of dreams, but one of very tragic realities. It is under the brazen sky of Africa, the Africa that belongs to France, and which perhaps for that very reason we French people know so little about, that the action of the book takes place. The hero, a type of African Don Juan, consumed by all the fires of concupiscence, recoils before nothing to satisfy his inordinate desires. . .· . .

The hero of the tragic revel and the horse of stone is not a more striking figure, nor his doom more unexpected. Such is the *motif* of the book. Add to this a warm rich style, and superb descriptive passages, these last abounding in local colour,—for the author speaks of the real Africa, as one who has seen it, and not as a mere novelist of vivid imagination,—and you will have some feeble idea of this book, this reflection of the East in its simple-hearted loves, its savage bursts of anger and its burning passions.

A. Z.

To appear in January a limited edition in one volume,
uniform with the "French Volunteer", of

THE ONLY BIOGRAPHY IN THE ENGLISH LANGUAGE

OF

SOPHIE ARNOULD

ACTRESS AND WIT

BY

R. B. DOUGLAS

WITH SEVEN COPPER-PLATE ENGRAVINGS

Expressly designed and etched for this work

BY

ADOLPHE LALAUZE

PARIS

CHARLES CARRINGTON

MDCCCXCVIII

SOPHIE ARNOULD

Amongst the great actresses of France none occupies, a position half so unique as that of the volatile courtesan called Sophie Arnould.

Gay as a butterfly on a midsummer's day, the mordant satire of her tongue stung like a wasp. She symbolised the spirit of Paris and of Comedy at a period when the Comedy and Paris had attained their most brilliant culmination. Her satire was unstudied and her jests of the lightest, when levity and irony were most cultivated. From the sublime to the absurd, and from the absurd to the sublime, she soared or fell in the same instant with equal wit and facility. She was easily the first among the first and most famous actresses of her time.

The Goncourt brothers have well remarked the rarity of such creatures as was Sophie Arnould. She is the legitimate successor of the immortal actress-courtesans of the past, Aspasia, Imperia or Ninon. These women are the gracious and frank confession of the Manners and Ideas of their epoch; in their biographies we find the disrobed and intimate life of the generation which they intoxicated with their wit. To them we owe those memories of enchantment of the centuries that have gone; and in the story of their lives the golden ages of Pericles, Leo X, Louis XIV, and the pre-Revolution period, live and move again before us in all their splendour.

Great men, heroes, captains, and kings we can do without—these other children of Love, Venus and Fortune—NEVER.

The attention of Book-lovers is called
TO THE FOLLOWING CURIOUS AND HIGHLY
INTERESTING WORK

Now ready for delivery

THE

Curious Bypaths of History

FOLLOWED BY A FASCINATING STUDY OF

Flagellation in France

From a Literary, Medical, and Historical Standpoint

With special FOREWORD by the Editor dealing with
the Reviewers of a previous work, and sundry other
cognate matters good to be known; particularly concerning
certain high-handed proceedings of BRITISH PHILISTINISM.

A fine Copper-plate Frontispiece after a Design by DANIEL VIERGE

(Engraved by F. MASSÉ)

The whole in One Volume on specially made, stout,
white, VAN GELDER, vellum paper.   **Price 21s.**

Until December (1897), *after which date the price will be*
40 fr. net

N.B.—With this book will be given (*under cover*) a fine Plate
entitled: CONJUGAL CORRECTION reproduced in
AQUATINTE by the MAISON GOUPIL (of Paris) after the
famous OIL PAINTING of CORREGGIO.

This book appeals to all classes. The Scholar will find in it
a mine of information mostly new; the Bibliophile will prize it
for its "get up"; and the "general reader" will be struck with
its quaint old-world charm and real curiousness.

"Bonheur d'aujourd'hui! Bonheur d'aujourd'hui! Gardons-le, quand nous le tenons; enfermons-le dans notre cœur comme l'amour de la bien-aimée et ne le livrons pas aux caprices et aux incertitudes de ce ravisseur avide et changeant qui s'appelle: "Demain"! (Page 97.)